I0190260

THE TRANSFORMATIVE POWER OF YOUR FAMILY ALTAR

David Philemon

Royal Diadem Publishing Inc.

Copyright © 2024 David Philemon

All rights reserved. First Edition 2024.
Printed in the USA.

Published by David Philemon and Royal Diadem Publishing Inc.

All rights reserved under International Copyright Law. No part of this book may be reproduced, stored in a retrieval system, or transmitted in any form or by any means, electronic, mechanical, photocopying, recording, or otherwise, the express written permission from the author and publisher. Unauthorized use or distribution of this material is strictly prohibited.

Breaking Barriers
The Transformative Power of Your Family Altar
978-1-966141-44-0

For permissions, additional information, or bulk order inquiries, please contact the author.

Write:
Royal Diadem Publishing Inc.
4836 W. 13th Street, Cicero, IL 60804
1 (312) 970-0183

Unless otherwise indicated, all Scripture quotations in this volume are taken from the King James Version (KJV) and the New King James Version (NKJV) of the Holy Bible.

Dedication

To the Almighty God, my Rock, Refuge, and Source of all wisdom and strength. Thank You for Your unwavering love, grace, and the purpose You've placed within me. May this book bring glory to Your name and draw others closer to You.

And to my beloved spiritual parents, Dr. Paul and Dr. Mrs. Becky Paul Enenche, who have faithfully nurtured and guided me in this journey. Your example of unwavering devotion, godly counsel, and compassionate care has been a beacon of light and strength in my life. Thank you for standing as pillars of faith and for your steadfast commitment to the Kingdom.

ACKNOWLEDGMENTS

This book would not have been possible without the unwavering support, dedication, and talent of an extraordinary team. My deepest gratitude goes to each of you for your contributions, insights, and encouragement throughout this journey.

First and foremost, thank you to Rev. Mimi Philemon my dear wife, Rev. Shina Gentry, and and my assistant pastor Rev. Bright Amudoaghan for your incredible effort, encouragement, and belief in this project. Your support has been instrumental in bringing this vision to life.

To the dedicated leaders of Royal Diadem Publishing, Ide Imogie and Kishawna Bailey, I am immensely grateful for your belief in this project from the very beginning and for investing your time and energy into its development. Your creativity, dedication, and expertise have been the backbone of this endeavor.

I am especially grateful to the Royal Diadem Publishing team—Beulah Orogun, Emmanuella Ben-Eboh, Doyinsade Awodele, Kim Matthews, and Shante Gill, for your meticulous attention to detail, refining every page and ensuring that each word reflects our vision.

A heartfelt thank you to my family, friends, and colleagues whose unwavering support and belief in this project gave me the courage and strength to see it through.

Finally, thank you to all the readers and supporters who make this work meaningful. I am humbled and honored to share this journey with each of you.

With all my gratitude,
David Philemon

CONTENTS

APOSTLE DR. DAVID PHILEMON

INTRODUCTION

Have you ever wondered how you can unleash the power of the spirit realm in all that concerns you and see God's power conquer devils, break curses, and turn your life around? Have you been going through several challenges and demonic oppressions, but the enemy seems to always be above you? It is time to understand the system God has made available for your victory, no matter what you are going through. I am talking about the power of altars.

In the pages of this book, I will take you on a journey of discovery, unearthing the great spiritual truths about altars hidden in plain sight throughout the scriptures. The revelation of altars is not new; it is as old as man's relationship with God. From Adam and Eve through the patriarchs and prophets and into the New Testament era, altars have played a crucial role in man's interaction with the spirit realms. Nevertheless, what exactly is an altar? In its simplest form, an altar is a place of exchange between the natural and the supernatural realms. It is a point of contact where heaven touches Earth and the seen and unseen converge.

The Bible contains numerous accounts of altars serving as focal points for divine encounters, miraculous interventions, and spiritual breakthroughs. Understanding the power of altars is crucial for every believer who desires to walk in victory and fulfill their God-given destiny. It is more significant than erecting physical structures; it is about creating spiritual landing pads through which God's presence and power can manifest in our daily lives. Imagine countering every enemy attack with the power of a well-maintained altar. Imagine breaking free from generational curses, overcoming stubborn habits, and entering in a new level of authority and anointing. That potential lies within the proper understanding and application of the power of altars.

Are you ready to discover the power of altars? Are you prepared to step into a new dimension of spiritual authority as an individual and in your family? Then, let us embark on this life-changing journey together.

CHAPTER ONE

UNDERSTANDING THE MYSTERY OF ALTARS

What Is An Altar?

An altar is essentially a raised area in a structure that is devoted to God or any other demonic or satanic force. The thing that many people overlook is that altars are more than just the raised monument's physical structure. An altar is a bridge through which the spirit realm can invade our realm. Without an altar, no spirit has a legal ground to operate on the earth. So, an altar is like a spiritual runway or a landing pad through which spirits can land on earth. When you begin to understand this, you will see the necessity and power of altars in our walk with God.

When a demonic altar is raised against you, there is nothing in the natural you will ever be able to do to fight back because you are not fighting a human being; you are rather fighting a system that has empowered spirits to invade your space.

Let me give you another definition to deepen your understanding. "An altar is a supernatural system of authorization for the spirit realm to have entrance and encounter with the physical realm". If you have tried to travel before, then you know the rigors of getting a passport and visiting the immigration office, all so you can get authorization to step into a territory. This is exactly what an altar is. It grants you access to step into the spirit world, interact with spirit beings, bargain with them, and then authorize them, if necessary, according to your demands for them to invade the natural realm.

The mystery of altars is deeply rooted in biblical history and plays a crucial role in the spiritual dynamics of both the Old and New Testaments. In Genesis 8:20 (KJV), we read, "And Noah builded an altar unto the LORD; and took of every clean beast, and of every clean fowl, and offered burnt offerings on the altar." The verses indicate that as soon as he raised this altar, the Lord gave him an audience and granted his request. This demonstrates one of the earliest examples of altar construction in the Bible and emphasizes its significance in forging a bond between man and God.

Another way to understand it is that altars serve as contact points between the natural and supernatural realms. They are spiritual gateways facilitating communication and interaction between humans and the divine. This understanding is crucial for you as a believer who seeks to deepen your relationship with God and effectively navigate the spiritual landscape. Read Exodus 20:24 (KJV), you will see that God instructed the Israelites saying: "An altar of earth thou shalt make unto me, and shalt sacrifice thereon thy burnt offerings, and thy peace offerings, thy sheep, and thine oxen: in all places where I record my name, I will come unto thee, and I will bless thee." Now, this scripture shows us the importance of altars as places of sacrifice and divine encounters. Through these altars, God promises to meet with His people and bestow His blessings upon them.

Spiritual Amplifiers

The power of altars goes beyond mere religious rituals; they serve as spiritual amplifiers, intensifying the potency of prayers, sacrifices, and declarations made upon them. Throughout scripture, we see individuals and nations erecting altars at pivotal moments in their spiritual journeys. For instance, in 1 Kings

18:30-32 (KJV), we witness Elijah repairing the altar of the Lord before his iconic showdown with the prophets of Baal: "And Elijah said unto all the people, Come near unto me. And all the people came near unto him. And he repaired the altar of the LORD that was broken down. And Elijah took twelve stones, according to the number of the tribes of the sons of Jacob, unto whom the word of the LORD came, saying, Israel shall be thy name: And with the stones he built an altar in the name of the LORD: and he made a trench about the altar, as great as would contain two measures of seed."

This act of repairing and consecrating the altar was instrumental in the miraculous demonstration of God's power that followed; without it, I can assure you that Elijah would not have seen the power of God. It is a powerful reminder of the strategic importance of altars in spiritual warfare and divine interventions. Also, altars are not limited to physical structures. Read the New Testament; it expands our understanding of altars to include our hearts and lives as living sacrifices. Romans 12:1 (KJV) says, "I beseech you therefore, brethren, by the mercies of God, that ye present your bodies a living sacrifice, holy, acceptable unto God, which is your reasonable service." This transformation of the concept of altars from external structures to internal consecration emphasizes the personal and intimate nature of our relationship with God in the new covenant.

If this is not understood, you run the risk of falling prey to a lot of the enemy's circumstances. Understanding the nature and function of altars is crucial for every believer who desires to walk in spiritual authority and experience the fullness of God's presence and power.

Altars are not mere religious symbols or archaic practices; they are dynamic spiritual tools that can revolutionize our prayer life, worship, and overall spiritual effectiveness when properly understood and utilized. In spiritual warfare, altars are pivotal because they can be used as strongholds of divine protection or, conversely, as points of demonic influence. This dual nature of altars shows us the importance of discernment and spiritual vigilance. As believers, we must be aware of the altars that exist in our lives, families, and communities, ensuring that they are consecrated to God and not serving as access points for malevolent spiritual forces.

Altars and Destinies

The power of altars in shaping destinies is crucial and cannot be overstated. Read the scriptures, you will see that throughout scripture, altars became turning points in the lives of individuals and nations. Consider it: Abraham's willingness to sacrifice Isaac on Mount Moriah (Genesis 22:9-14, KJV) not only tested his faith but also established a mighty altar that would later become the site of Solomon's temple. This altar became a generational point of blessing and divine encounter. Understanding altars helps us recognize the spiritual significance of our decisions, actions, and commitments in our modern context. This means that every time we dedicate our lives, resources, or endeavors to God, we are essentially raising an altar. Do you get it? Furthermore, these spiritual altars become focal points of divine activity in our lives, attracting God's presence and repelling enemy forces.

Knowledge of altars will help you to understand the power of consecration and separation unto God. In a world filled with competing influences and distractions, erecting personal and family altars of worship, prayer, and dedication to God is a powerful means of aligning ourselves with divine purposes and protecting our spiritual inheritance.

As we keep going deeper into this subject of altars, it will become evident to you that they are not just religious artifacts of the past but living and dynamic spiritual realities that continue to shape the landscape of our lives and daily experiences Whether physical or spiritual, family or individual, personal or corporate, altars remain central to our interaction with the divine and our effectiveness in battling the demonic.

Altars And Manipulation Of Destinies

Delilah's Manipulation, Judges 16:15-18

Samson's life is a profound illustration of how altars can manipulate destinies, even when God is involved in a person's life. Chosen by God from birth and given supernatural strength did not prevent Samson's life from ending in destruction. This tragic outcome was not the result of confrontation or physical overpowering, but rather through subtle manipulation. The powers that could not defeat Samson through force found success through deception and manipulation, and this shows us the treacherous nature of demonic altars in spiritual warfare.

In Judges 16:15 (TLB), we see a pivotal moment in this manipulation: *"Then Delilah said to Samson, 'How can you say you love me when you don't confide in me? You have made fun of me three times now, and you still haven't told me what makes you so strong!'"* Delilah's seemingly innocent question masks a deeper and more devilish agenda at work. Delilah's words were not merely those of a curious lover, but the manifestation of a carefully orchestrated plan rooted in demonic altars, which the Philistines must have raised.

Many must comprehend that spiritual altars are constantly at work behind the scenes. The events we witness in the natural realm are often not purely natural occurrences but the result of spiritual altars manipulating lives and destinies. This unseen spiritual activity explains why many individuals are trapped in destructive patterns or facing inexplicable setbacks. The manipulation of destinies through altars is the primary reason why countless lives are destroyed in terrible ways, often leaving observers perplexed at the apparent senselessness of these tragedies.

Samson's downfall exemplifies this principle; his extraordinary strength was not just a physical attribute but a spiritual endowment, symbolized by the uncut hair sign of his Nazirite vow. This vow was a spiritual altar, a covenant between Samson and God that was the source of his strength. Delilah's persistent questioning was an attack on this altar, aimed at dismantling the very foundation of Samson's power and purpose, but he never knew; however, the moment he opened his mouth, he polluted his altar.

The gravity of this situation becomes more apparent when reading Judges 16:16-17 (KJV): *"And it came to pass, when she pressed him daily with her words, and urged him, so that his soul was vexed unto death; That he told her all his heart, and said unto her, There hath not come a razor upon mine head; for I have been a Nazarite unto God from my mother's womb: if I be shaven, then my strength will go from me, and I shall become weak, and be like any other man."* Can you see the relentless nature of the attack on Samson's altar? Delilah's daily pressing was not merely an annoying persistence but a sustained assault on Samson's spiritual defenses. The phrase "his soul was vexed unto death" shows us the profound spiritual and emotional toll this manipulation took on Samson. It was not just irritation but a wearing down of his very being, identity, and connection to God.

When Samson finally revealed the secret of his strength, he wasn't just sharing information, he was surrendering the altar of his Nazirite vow and this act of disclosure was tantamount to dismantling the divine altar in his life and allowing a demonic altar to erect in its place. The consequences were immediate and severe, as we see in Judges 16:18-20 (KJV): *"And when Delilah saw that he had told her all his heart, she sent and called for the lords of the Philistines, saying, Come up this once, for he hath shewed me all his heart. Then the lords of the Philistines came up unto her, and brought money in their hand. And she made him sleep upon her knees; and she called for a man, and she caused him to shave off the seven locks of his head; and she began to afflict him, and his strength went from him. And she said, The Philistines be upon thee, Samson. And he awoke out of his sleep, and said, I will go out as at other times before, and shake myself. And he wist not that the LORD was departed from him."*

This scripture shows us a vivid picture of the transfer of spiritual authority. The moment Samson's hair was cut, the altar of his strength was demolished, and a new altar of bondage and defeat was established. The phrase "he knew not that the LORD was departed from him" simply lets us know that his altar was no longer sufficient to protect him. Because altars are the platform through which spirits can enter this realm to participate in our lives, the Lord had to leave Samson because His altar was no longer functional.

In that same book of Judges, we have a different example of altars being positively used to manipulate destinies for good. We have a woman named Deborah, a prophetess and judge of Israel. Unlike Samson, who fell victim to manipulation, Deborah used her understanding of spiritual principles to bring about deliverance and advance God's kingdom. Judges 4:4-5 (KJV) says, *"And Deborah, a prophetess, the wife of Lapidoth, she judged Israel at that time. And she dwelt under the palm tree of Deborah between Ramah and Bethel in mount Ephraim: and the children of Israel came up to her for judgment."* Deborah's dwelling under the palm tree was more than just a physical location; it was a spiritual altar from which she exercised her authority and dispensed godly wisdom.

Deborah's role in Israel's deliverance from Jabin, king of Canaan, demonstrates how a divine altar can be used to manipulate destinies for good. In Judges 4:6-7 (KJV), we see her calling Barak to lead the army: *"And she sent and called Barak the son of Abinoam out of Kedeshnaphtali, and said unto him, Hath not the LORD God of Israel commanded, saying, Go and draw toward mount Tabor, and take with thee ten thousand men of the children of Naphtali and of the children of Zebulun? And I will draw unto thee to the river Kishon Sisera, the captain of Jabin's army, with his chariots and his multitude; and I will deliver him into thine hand."*

Deborah's words were not mere military strategy, but prophetic declarations rooted in her connection to God's altar. She established a divine altar of victory over Israel's enemies by speaking these words. Her partnership with Barak in this endeavor shows how godly manipulation of destinies often involves collaboration and the empowerment of others.

The contrast between Samson's and Deborah's stories shows us a great truth about altars and the manipulation of destinies. While demonic altars seek to destroy and enslave, divine altars empower and liberate. Samson's strength was impressive, but he ultimately failed when he allowed his altar to be compromised. On the other hand, Deborah operated from a place of wisdom and divine connection, using her authority to raise others and bring about national deliverance.

This comparison teaches that the most effective defense against manipulating demonic altars is a solid and collective divine altar, not individual might. This is why we are discussing family altars in this book. You may be strong on your own, but when your whole family can erect an effective altar, you can be sure that nothing will ever be able to defeat you.

The manipulation of destinies through altars is a reality you must be aware of and prepared to confront. Anyone who says that altars are not real is indeed joking; in fact, they are probably being manipulated by one. Be vigilant in maintaining your divine altars through prayer, obedience, and commitment to God's word while ensuring that your family altar is solid and powerful. What is the use of being able to save yourself, but your family is left in trouble because they do not have an altar speaking for them in the realm of the Spirit? Think about this!

The Biblical Foundation Of Altars

Throughout scripture, we see altars playing pivotal roles in the spiritual lives of individuals and nations, serving as points of divine encounter, sacrifice, and covenant-making. One of the most striking examples of the positive power of altars is f in the story of Samuel and the Philistines. In 1 Samuel 7:9-10 (KJV) says, *"And Samuel took a sucking lamb, and offered it for a burnt offering wholly unto the LORD: and Samuel cried unto the LORD for Israel; and the LORD heard him. And as Samuel was offering up the burnt offering, the Philistines drew near to battle against Israel: but the LORD thundered with a great thunder on that day upon the Philistines, and discomfited them; and they were smitten before Israel."*

Wow, think of the immense power an altar can release! The people were coming to fight the Israelites, but Samuel knew the power of altars, and the moment he offered a sacrifice, thunder was upon their enemy. When you understand the power of altars, no enemy will ever be able to stand against you. This incident powerfully demonstrates how an altar, when used in accordance with God's will, can turn the tide of battle and bring about divine intervention. Samuel's sacrifice on the altar was not merely a religious ritual; it was a spiritual catalyst that invited God's power into their dire situation. The thundering of the Lord that followed was a direct response to the altar Samuel had raised, showcasing how altars can serve as conduits for supernatural manifestations.

Balak and Balam (Altars of Blessings and Curses)

On the other hand, the Bible also provides examples of altars used for demonic and dark purposes. The story of Balak and Balaam in Numbers 22–24 is a clear example and reminder. Balak, the King of Moab, sought to curse Israel, so he employed the services of the prophet Balaam. In Numbers 23:1-2 (KJV), the Bible shows us their attempts: *"And Balaam said unto Balak, Build me here seven altars, and prepare me here seven oxen and seven rams. And Balak did as Balaam had spoken; and Balak and Balaam offered on every altar a bullock and a ram."* This shows us how even those with spiritual knowledge can attempt to use altars for purposes contrary to God's will. The repeated construction of altars, seven in total, shows the intensity of their efforts to manipulate spiritual forces against Israel. Take a moment to imagine raising seven altars. God's sovereignty prevailed, and Balaam blessed Israel instead of cursing them, proving that no altar raised against God's people could prosper when they were under divine protection. Why did the Curse of Balam not work? It was not because the children of Israel were nice people; it was because they had a higher altar in the realm of the Spirit. Their altar was speaking blessings over them.

The King Of Moab (Sacrifice on the Altar)

Another example of altars at work is in 2 Kings 3:26-27 (KJV), where we read about the King of Moab sacrificing his firstborn son on the wall as a burnt offering. This desperate act, performed on what was essentially an impromptu altar, had immediate and severe consequences. The Bible says, *"And when the king of Moab saw that the battle was too sore for him, he took with him seven hundred men that drew swords, to break through even unto the king of Edom: but they could not. Then he took his eldest son that should have reigned in his stead, and offered him for a burnt offering upon the wall. And there was great indignation against Israel: and they departed from him, and returned to their own land."*

In case you do not know the background of this story, The Moabites were in battle against the children of Israel, and unfortunately, they were losing while Israel was winning. So what did the King do? The Bible reveals that he immediately took his son, who was next to be king, and he sacrificed Him; this sacrifice, made in desperation, was powerful and strengthened the altars backing the Moabites, turning the tide of the battle against Israel. This should serve as an excellent reminder always and remind you of the tremendous power that can be invoked through altars, even if it is a demonic altar. Also, this incident should teach you the gravity with which you must approach the altars and sacrifices, recognizing their potential for both good and evil.

Elijah on The Mount

On a positive note, the story of Elijah on Mount Carmel (1 Kings

18:20–40) provides one of the most dramatic demonstrations of the power of a divinely sanctioned altar. In a showdown with the prophets of Baal, Elijah repaired the altar of the Lord and prepared a sacrifice. His prayer at this altar resulted in fire from heaven consuming not only the sacrifice but the altar itself, along with the water poured around it. This spectacular display of God's power through an altar led to a national revival and the turning of hearts back to the true God.

The New Testament does not abandon the revelation of altars but transforms it. Although physical altars are less necessary in the New Testament, the principle of sacrifice and dedication remains very important. Hebrews 13:10 (KJV) reveals a spiritual altar: *"We have an altar, whereof they have no right to eat, which serve the tabernacle."* This altar is understood to be Christ Himself, the ultimate sacrifice that has transformed how we understand and interact with altars under the New Covenant. To truly understand altars in the New Testament, look at Romans 12:1 (KJV): *"I beseech you therefore, brethren, by the mercies of God, that ye present your bodies a living sacrifice, holy, acceptable unto God, which is your reasonable service."* This verse turns every one of us who are believers into a walking and breathing altar, which is God's intention.

It is not about having an altar; the Lord wants you to become the altar in the New Testament. Do you also know what? Your life is the greatest sacrifice you will offer on that altar.

In essence, the biblical foundation of altars is multifaceted and profound. From the patriarchs to the prophets, from kings to ordinary people, altars have served as points of encounter with the divine, instruments of warfare and symbols of dedication. They have been used for righteous and unrighteous purposes, demonstrating the need for discernment and reverence in spiritual matters.

Different Types Of Altars

The Divine And The Demonic

When we talk about the divine, we are talking about light, the heavenly realm, the angelic realm, and all that the Holy Spirit powers. But when we are talking about the demonic realm, we are talking about Satan and all other demons that work for him. This means that before you understand altars, you must know there are divine and demonic altars. These demonic altars are very terrible. Many times, when you see tears, destruction, wickedness, pain, death, and so much more, you need to know that these things do not just happen. Only a demonic altar releasing wicked and demonic spirits can make it possible. But then, when you see deliverance, hope, love, generosity, salvation, kindness, progress, and healing, it means so many angelic activities are happening because a godly altar somewhere is being raised and authorizing the divine realm to invade our worl

Divine Altars are those consecrated to the Almighty God; they serve as points of contact between heaven and earth, facilitating the flow of God's power, presence, and blessings into our realm. In Exodus 20:24 (KJV), God instructs, "An altar of earth thou shalt make unto me, and shalt sacrifice thereon thy burnt offerings, and thy peace offerings, thy sheep, and thine oxen: in all places where I record my name, I will come unto thee, and I will bless thee." This verse encapsulates the essence of divine altars, where God promises to meet with His people and bless them.

You must also know that divine altars are characterized by righteousness, purity, and holiness. They are built and maintained through prayer, worship, obedience to God's word, and sacrificial living. When believers consistently seek God's face, study His word, and live in obedience, they erect a divine altar in their lives. This altar becomes a conduit for God's power and presence, not just in their personal lives but also in their surroundings.

2 Chronicles 7:1-3 (KJV) is a powerful example of a divine altar in action. The Bible says, *"Now when Solomon had made an end of*

praying, the fire came down from heaven, and consumed the burnt offering and the sacrifices, and the glory of the LORD filled the house. And the priests could not enter into the house of the LORD, because the glory of the LORD had filled the LORD'S house. And when all the children of Israel saw how the fire came down, and the glory of the LORD upon the house, they bowed themselves with their faces to the ground upon the pavement, and worshipped, and praised the LORD, saying, For he is good; for his mercy endureth forever." This bible passage shows us the incredible power and manifestation at a divine altar. The altar Solomon had built became a focal point for God's glory to descend, resulting in nationwide revival and worship.

On the other hand, demonic altars are spiritual structures dedicated to Satan and his cohorts, which serve as entry points for evil forces to operate in the physical realm, often resulting in oppression, sickness, failure, and various forms of bondage. Demonic altars can be established through idolatry, occult practices, generational sins, or even ignorant participation in ungodly activities. In 2 Kings 21:2-5 (KJV), we have an example of the establishment of demonic altars *"And he did that which was evil in the sight of the LORD, after the abominations of the heathen, whom the LORD cast out before the children of Israel. For he built up again the high places which Hezekiah his father had destroyed; and he reared up altars for Baal, and made a grove, as did Ahab king of Israel; and worshipped all the host of heaven, and served them. And he built altars in the house of the LORD, of which the LORD said, In Jerusalem will I put my name. And he built altars for all the host of heaven in the two courts of the house of the LORD."*

This passage describes how King Manasseh of Judah erected altars to false gods, effectively establishing demonic altars that brought great evil upon the nation. The consequences of these actions were severe, leading to captivity and suffering for the people of Judah. Demonic altars operate through deception, fear, and bondage. They often masquerade as sources of power or prosperity but ultimately lead to destruction. In 1 Corinthians

10:20 (KJV), Paul warns, "But I say, that the things which the Gentiles sacrifice, they sacrifice to devils, and not to God: and I would not that ye should have fellowship with devils." This verse underscores the reality that engaging with demonic altars, even ignorantly, opens doors to demonic influence and oppression.

It is imperative to understand that the battle between divine and demonic altars is always ongoing in the spiritual realm, and nothing will change that. As long as we believers can pray, worship, and live as Christians and as long as wicked and unreasonable people will not change their ways but instead continue to walk in darkness, the fight between the demonic and divine altar will always remain. Ephesians 6:12 (KJV) says, *"For we wrestle not against flesh and blood, but against principalities, against powers, against the rulers of the darkness of this world, against spiritual wickedness in high places."* This spiritual warfare often manifests as a clash between divine and demonic altars.

Practically, a family consistently devoted to prayer, studying God's word, and righteous living maintains a divine altar that will provide spiritual protection and invite God's blessings. Meanwhile, a household given to constant strife, immorality, or occult practices will unknowingly erect demonic altars that invite chaos and destruction.

Now that you understand the different types of altars, you must become more intentional about your spiritual life. It calls for vigilance in guarding against the establishment of demonic altars while actively building and maintaining divine altars, not just personally but in your family. It teaches you to recognize the reality of demonic altars and motivates you to engage in strategic spiritual warfare every day because whether you like it or not, there is warfare going on, and you are a big part of it

THE SIGNIFICANCE OF ALTARS IN SPIRITUAL WARFARE

The power of altars in warfare lies in the fact that destinies and outcomes in the natural realm can be manipulated through altars. In Judges 16:18 (MSG), the bible shows us a clear example of this saying *"When Delilah realized that he had told her his secret, she sent for the Philistine tyrants, telling them, 'Come quickly—this time he's told me the truth.' The Philistine tyrants came, bringing the silver with them."* Do you see it? This is how contradictory altars can manipulate a life, causing someone to become weak and submit to the very causes of their destruction.

This spiritual principle explains many perplexing behaviors we observe in people's lives. This is why you can see a man dying of liver disease but can't say no to alcohol, or someone dying of diabetes but can't resist sugary foods, or perhaps you have seen someone dying of lung cancer but unable to quit smoking. These aren't just about lack of willpower; they often indicate a more in-depth spiritual manipulation at work. Demonic agents that altars have authorized to destroy lives are the reason why you see them doing things that are destructive to them.

Have you also thought about the tragic situations where some people remain in abusive relationships, seemingly unable to break free? They would rather stay in a death trap than face life alone. It is often a sign of spiritual manipulation through altars; something wicked is at work and has been raised to power by forces beyond the natural realm.

Strategic Points of Power

In spiritual warfare, altars also serve as strategic points of power; this means they are like spiritual command centers from which battles are won or lost. This is why, in many biblical accounts of warfare, we see altars playing a crucial role. For example, the story of Gideon in Judges 6. Before Gideon could lead Israel to victory against the Midianites, he had first to tear down the altar of Baal and build an altar to the Lord (Judges 6:25-26, KJV): "And it came to pass the same night, that the LORD said unto him, Take thy father's young bullock, even the second bullock of seven years old, and throw down the altar of Baal that thy father hath, and cut down the grove that is by it: And build an altar unto the LORD thy God upon the top of this rock, in the ordered place, and take the second bullock, and offer a burnt sacrifice with the wood of the grove which thou shalt cut down."

The demolishing of the demonic altar and erecting a divine one was the first step in Israel's deliverance. It broke the spiritual stronghold the Midianites had over the land and paved the way for God's power to manifest.

Similarly, in 1 Kings 18, which we talked about earlier, we see the epic showdown between Elijah and the prophets of Baal on Mount Carmel. The entire contest revolved around altars; they were battling which altar could bring down fire from heaven. This wasn't just a display of supernatural power but a decisive spiritual battle that would determine the course of Israel's spiritual allegiance.

Each time I look around, I see so many believers find themselves fighting battles in the natural realm against sickness, financial lack, relational strife, devilish habits, and so much more, without realizing that the real fight is in the spiritual realm because altars are raised against them and they have no altars to help them fight back. Just as in Gideon's time, victory began with identifying and demolishing demonic altars while establishing and strengthening divine ones; I want you to know you will only go far with having an altar to back you up against the several altars that are desperate to destroy you.

For instance, a family struggling with constant conflict and disunity might be dealing with the effects of a demonic altar, perhaps erected through generational sins or curses. The solution is not better communication or anger management techniques (this will only help if the situation is purely natural), but the real breakthrough comes when they identify the spiritual root, renounce any connections to demonic altars, and intentionally establish a family altar fueled by prayer, worship, and a burning dedication to God.

In 2 Corinthians 10:4-5 (KJV), Paul gives us insight into the nature of this warfare when he said, *"For the weapons of our warfare are not carnal, but mighty through God to the pulling down of strong holds; Casting down imaginations, and every high thing that exalteth itself against the knowledge of God, and bringing into captivity every thought to the obedience of Christ."* These strongholds often operate through altars; our spiritual weapons are designed to identify and demolish these altars.

The significance of altars in spiritual warfare cannot be overstated. They are the fronts on which major spiritual battles are fought and won. By understanding this, you will be able to engage more effectively in spiritual warfare, not just fighting symptoms but addressing root causes because through the power of Christ, we have the authority to tear down demonic altars and establish divine ones, change the spiritual atmosphere around us and pave the way for God's kingdom to manifest in our lives and communities but we must first of all have our altars in place, because if you engage in warfare without an altar you will end up becoming a casualty.

WHY YOUR FAMILY NEEDS AN ALTAR

The family is one of the most powerful units; do you know that? Every life starts with a family, and the family unit has the most significant influence on every life, especially during the formative years of that life. This means that to attack somebody, it starts with the family. The devil knows this, demonic agents know this, and every agent of the demonic realm knows this! Therefore, no family is truly safe if they do not have an altar! But with a family altar, your family is secured, and you will mobilize spiritual resources to your advantage because you can see the power of God released when the need arises. Note this: When altars manipulate destinies, things fall apart until they are disintegrated.

Think about Samson once more. People were not usually patient with prostitutes in those days, so why were they patient with

Delilah? This is because the element manipulating the whole happenings came from the altars of the Philistines and was stronger than the altar of Samson. Do not forget Samson's life started on the altar of God, with an angel of the Lord telling the mother, "You will have a baby." The mother told the husband, and she prayed. When she prayed, the angel returned the next day to speak with her husband. After receiving instructions, the man wanted to bring the angel a meal, but the angel said, even if I stay, I will not eat, but if you are going to give God an offering, give him a whole burnt offering. Why are all these prayers and sacrifices necessary? They strengthened the family altar and prepared the family for what God would do by bringing Samson into the family. If your family lacks an altar, you may never see your prophecies fulfilled.

In Judges 13:16 (MSG), the bible says, *"And the angel of the LORD said unto Manoah, Though thou detain me, I will not eat of thy bread: and if thou wilt offer a burnt offering, thou must offer it unto the LORD. For Manoah knew not that he was an angel of the LORD."* This passage teaches us a great truth: you can never say to God, "My heart belongs to you," when your cash belongs to you. Some people give to God, but they haven't come to a place where God strips them; they haven't come to a place where they can provide something that will cost them. And that is the place of glory; it may look as if you don't have sense when you give dangerous sacrifices like that, but wait for that season to turn, and you will realize that the strength of your sacrifice releases very great power on your altar.

A Quick Overview of Why You Need An Altar

- **Bringing Prophecies To Come To Pass**
- When dealing with heavy-duty prophecy, you must ensure your altar is sanctified and satisfied. This means you must learn to make great sacrifices that

touch your heart and sometimes even feel very painful. Do not think you are losing when you do this; no, you are not! You are creating a powerful system around you and your family that will protect and provide for you, fight for you, and ensure that no evil can touch you. I can assure you that in today's world, where wickedness seems to reign everywhere, you need an altar.

- **Your Fortress & Spiritual Protection**
- The necessity of a family altar cannot be overstated. In today's world, where families face unprecedented challenges and attacks from various quarters. A family altar is your spiritual fortress, refuge, and a source of divine guidance and protection. It's more than having a physical space in your home dedicated to prayer and worship (although that can be helpful). Instead, it's about cultivating a consistent, intentional practice of seeking God together as a family. Psalm 127:1 (KJV) says, *"Except the LORD build the house, they labour in vain that build it: except the LORD keep the city, the watchman waketh but in vain."* This verse captures the futility of protecting and prospering your family without God's involvement. You will see them destroyed and torn into pieces in front of your eyes, but a family altar invites God's power, dominion, angelic assistance, presence, and protection over your household.
- Look at the life of Job for example, in Job 1:5 (KJV), the bible says, *"And it was so, when the days of their feasting were gone about, that Job sent and sanctified them, and rose up early in the morning, and offered burnt offerings according to the number of them all: for Job said, It may be that my sons have sinned, and cursed God in their hearts. Thus did Job continually."* Job was a man of altars; he consistently offered sacrifices for his family and maintained the family altar. This altar

was why the devil could never touch him; it served as a protective hedge around his family, so much so that even when Satan wanted to attack Job, he was complaining to God that God's protection around Job was too much, so do you want to enjoy protection in your family? Take altars and sacrifices seriously!

- **Activation of Generational Blessings**
- Another crucial reason for establishing a family altar is for generational blessings. In Exodus 20:6 (KJV), God said, *"And shewing mercy unto thousands of them that love me, and keep my commandments."* This promise of generational blessing is activated through consistent devotion to God, facilitated by a family altar. When you establish a tradition of seeking God together, you are not just impacting your immediate family but laying a foundation for future generations.
- **Family Instruction and Discipleship**
- A family altar also serves as a place of instruction and discipleship; this is why Deuteronomy 6:6-7 (KJV) commands, *"And these words, which I command thee this day, shall be in thine heart: And thou shalt teach them diligently unto thy children, and shalt talk of them when thou sittest in thine house, and when thou walkest by the way, and when thou liest down, and when thou risest up."* A family altar provides the perfect setting for consistent, everyday teaching of God's word. If you are not teaching your family the word and praying together, then you are not fulfilling God's demand for your life as a parent. You are setting your family up for destruction because the day the enemy attacks, everyone in that household would be vulnerable due to a lack of Spiritual discipline and an active altar that can protect them.
- **Strong Unity and Family Bond**
- A family altar promotes unity and strengthens family bonds; in a world where families are increasingly

fragmented, coming together regularly to seek God can be a powerful unifying force. It provides a safe space for open communication, shared vulnerability, and mutual support. Psalm 133:1 (KJV) says, *"Behold, how good and how pleasant it is for brethren to dwell together in unity!"* This unity, cultivated at the family altar, becomes a strength and a witness to the world.

- **Breaking Generational Curses**
- A family altar is also a potent tool for breaking generational curses and establishing new, godly patterns of blessings. I tell you the truth: many families are struggling with recurring issues, be it addiction, divorce, financial problems, or even health issues that seem to pass from one generation to the next. Do you know what this means? It means a curse or an altar has been activated to speak against that family. Only your family altar can become where these cycles can be broken through prayer, repentance, and intentional alignment with God's will.

- **Light In A Dark World**
- Also, a family altar prepares your household to be a beacon of light in a dark world. Jesus said in Matthew 5:14-16 (KJV), *"Ye are the light of the world. A city that is set on an hill cannot be hid. Neither do men light a candle, and put it under a bushel, but on a candlestick; and it giveth light unto all that are in the house. Let your light so shine before men, that they may see your good works, and glorify your Father which is in heaven."* When your family altar is functional and active, you will be able to raise a family that will forever be a shining light to the world and a proof to the world that not everyone can be "messed" with by the devil.
- In a time when families are under intense attack, establishing and maintaining a family altar is not just beneficial; it's your ticket to survival, and you must

not joke with it!

CHAPTER TWO

THE POWER OF A FAMILY ALTAR

Safeguarding The Destinies

P arents should be aware of their critical role in shaping their children's destinies, and this lack of understanding often leads to a casual approach towards spiritual matters, particularly in the realm of altars. But like I have been saying from chapter one, you must recognize that altars are not merely symbolic entities; they are powerful spiritual instruments that can significantly influence the course of one's life and the lives of future generations in tremendous ways. Altars are so real that even pagans recognize their potency and value; how much more do we who call upon the name of the living God? This is why we see various forms of altar-raising across different belief systems.

When altars are given the respect and attention they deserve, they function with remarkable precision, much like spiritual snipers. They carry out their divine assignments accurately, targeting areas of our lives that require divine intervention and transformation. These sacrifices on your altar must not be tokens of nice gestures or half-hearted offerings. Instead, they should represent your wholehearted devotion and commitment to God. As a child of God who wants to do business with altars, do not give God merely a portion of your life but offer Him your entire being.

As a parent, do all that you can to lay a strong spiritual foundation through your family altar for your children. Those who do this have positioned themselves to receive divine insights and direction concerning their children's destinies, and this spiritual sensitivity will enable them to correctly and spiritually order their children's steps in alignment with God's perfect will and purpose.

Let's talk about Samson's parents for a moment. The Angel of the Lord visited them, giving them instructions on how to raise their son. Judges 13:3-5 (KJV) tells us of this divine encounter: "And the Angel of the Lord appeared unto the woman, and said unto her, Behold now, thou art barren, and bearest not: but thou shalt conceive, and bear a son. ..... and no razor shall come on his head: for the child shall be a Nazarite unto God from the womb." This was a clear, divine mandate for Samson's life. Yet, later on, we find that Samson's life didn't reflect the magnitude of this calling. Why? Because his parents didn't introduce him to the power of their family altar. They failed to teach him how to connect with the God who had spoken about his life even before he was born.

Samson's parents had experienced the supernatural firsthand. The Angel appeared to them, not once but twice (Judges 13:9). Yet, there is no record that they brought Samson into this divine encounter. Why did Samson, a man whose birth was divinely announced, never call on this Angel during his lifetime? Where were his prayers, his moments of divine encounters? His parents failed to maintain that altar or failed to bring him to a point where he would realize the necessity of altars in his life, and as a result, Samson lived disconnected from the source of his power (GOD). The Bible shows us clearly that Samson's downfall wasn't just about his failures; it was a failure of the family altar.

How many parents are doing the same thing? We experience God's power and see His hand in our lives, but we fail to introduce our children to that same power of our family altar. Instead, we allow them to live life anyway because we think they are in a copter(?) age. Some of us don't even build altars in our homes. Instead, we focus on temporary things like education, careers, and material success. But what about their spiritual destiny? What about the divine calling God has placed on their lives?

My mother also had an encounter with an angel while I was in her womb, although she did not initially recognize him as such at that time. During her labor, approximately ten months after my conception, yes, I spent more than nine months in the womb; as I was saying, one day, she found herself alone while my father was away on a journey. In the early morning hours, around 4 AM, she ventured outside our house and was unexpectedly approached by a taxi driver. This occurrence was highly unusual, and the driver began to reveal details about the unborn child (myself) that he could not have known through any natural means. After taking my mother to the hospital, she attempted to pay the taxi driver for his services, but when she turned to do so, both the man and his vehicle disappeared without a trace. It is important to note that this was not a case of the car simply driving away; it had disappeared in a manner that defied natural explanation. She would have noticed it going away if it had driven away, but there was no sound or trace, and it just vanished.

Years later, after I had experienced personal salvation, I felt compelled to seek out the individual whom God had used to assist my mother and reveal information about my life. Through prayer and faith, God graciously answered this request, allowing me to connect with this divine being from my past. Such spiritual experiences were possible in our family due to my mother's commitment to maintaining an active altar. Her altar was continuously aflame with passion and adorned with sacrifices, creating an atmosphere conducive to divine visitations and revelations.

A Caution To Take Serious

Think about it: the first time Samson's mother saw the Angel, the father was not there, but they were able to bring the Angel back to speak with the father about Samson's destiny. This shows that it is possible to cultivate such an intimate relationship with God that the destinies of your children will become divinely protected and secured. The failure of Samson's parents lies not in their initial encounter with the divine messenger but in their apparent neglect to integrate Samson into the family's spiritual legacy and altar.

This oversight is a cautionary tale for parents today. They must recognize the importance of experiencing divine encounters, effectively communicating these experiences to their children, and intentionally involving them in the family's spiritual practices. The family altar should be a place of intergenerational worship, prayer, and spiritual instruction, where children are taught to recognize and respond to God's voice from an early age. If Samson had this, he would never have lost his life by falling on the altar of lust rather than on the family altar, which was meant to empower him in destiny.

As a parent know this and never forget it, your family altar extends beyond mere religious practices. It serves as a spiritual anchor for the entire household, creating an atmosphere where God's presence is tangible, and His guidance is sought in all matters. This consistent spiritual engagement is the platform through which destinies are secured, or your children will never be able to contend with the forces of darkness and Delilah that await them on the path of destiny. Your altar not only influences the immediate family but also future generations. As Psalm 78:4-6 (KJV) exhorts, *"We will not hide them from their children, shewing to the generation to come the praises of the Lord, and his strength, and his wonderful works that he hath done. For he established a testimony in Jacob, and appointed a law in Israel, which he commanded our fathers, that they should make them known to their children: That the generation to come might know them, even the children which should be born; who should arise and declare them to their children."*

Take time to think about it again. Why didn't Samson call on the Angel who appeared to his mother? Why did he lack divine guidance at crucial moments in his life? The answer is simple: his life had no ongoing, functional altar. A functional altar gives room for divine encounters, which leads to spiritual insight, protection, and a fulfillment of God's purpose. Parents, when you ignore the family altar, you not only fail God, but you also fail your children. Samson's parents failed him in this regard. Judges 13:22 (KJV) says, *"And Manoah said unto his wife, We shall surely die, because we have seen God."* They had encounters, they had instructions, yet there was no continuity. Do not be like them! You must intentionally and continuously invite the presence of God into your family's life. Your family altar should be the foundation for your children's spiritual journey, shaping their destiny and aligning them with God's will. If you neglect it, you will fail them, and the consequences will be devastating.

Altars Sponsor Encounters

The revelation that altars sponsor encounters is a profound truth that you must take time to reflect on and apply in your spiritual life. To fully understand the significance of this principle, you must first understand the nature of altars and their function in facilitating divine-human interactions. Throughout Scripture, we see numerous examples of altars as points of contact between God and His people, places where heaven touches the earth, and places where supernatural encounters occur. Amazingly, Samson's life once again serves as a cautionary tale in this regard.

Despite the extraordinary circumstances surrounding his birth and the divine purpose pronounced over his life, Samson never experienced a personal encounter with God or even the Angel who had appeared to his mother. This glaring omission in Samson's spiritual journey can be attributed to his absence of a powerful, functional altar. When you read the scriptures, you will see that Samson only prayed three times in his life. Wow! Isn't that a shame? Just by this alone, you can see that he never took spiritual things seriously and never had any encounter that would impact the fulfillment of his destiny. This paucity of prayer and lack of a consistent altar practice undoubtedly contributed to his eventual downfall and failure to realize his divine calling fully.

This should serve as a stark warning to every believer today about the dangers of neglecting our spiritual altars. If you find yourself living a life characterized by infrequent prayers and minimal engagement with God, you must recognize that you are placing yourself in a precarious position, one where the fulfillment of your destiny is at serious risk. The absence of a functional altar not only impacts your personal spiritual growth and destiny but also has far-reaching consequences for your families and future generations.

When we examine this issue on a familial level, the stakes become even higher because a family that lacks a vibrant, active altar is positioning itself in a place of vulnerability, exposed to potential destruction at any moment. This spiritual negligence will create an opening for the enemy to wreak havoc in their life and the lives of loved ones. This is why Peter said in 1 Peter 5:8 (KJV), *"Be sober, be vigilant; because your adversary the devil, as a roaring lion, walketh about, seeking whom he may devour."* Without a functional altar's protective covering and divine connection, your family is exposed to the enemy's attacks.

The Impact Is Unlimited

Consider the profound impact a single divine encounter can have on an individual's life and legacy. Abraham's encounter with God at Moriah's altar tested his faith and established a covenant that would impact nations for generations to come. Moses' encounter with God at the burning bush altar in the wilderness transformed him from a fugitive shepherd into the deliverer of Israel. David's encounters with God at various altars shaped him into a man after God's heart and a king whose lineage would eventually produce the Messiah.

These biblical examples show us the truth that altars sponsor encounters that have the power to define our destinies and shape the course of history. However, we must avoid falling into the trap of viewing these encounters as one-time events or rare occurrences reserved for biblical figures. The same God who met with Abraham, Moses, and David desires to have regular, intimate encounters with His children today. The key to experiencing these encounters is our commitment to maintaining active, functional altars in our lives and homes.

Now, look at your own life. Are you maintaining a family altar? Are you praying for your children, making sacrifices for them, and ensuring they have a spiritual foundation? If you do not, you are failing them. If Samson's parents had done this, Samson's story wouldn't have ended in tragedy. A family altar not only provides spiritual protection but also shapes the destiny of your children. Proverbs 22:6 (KJV) says, "Train up a child in the way he should go: and when he is old, he will not depart from it." But you can't train a child spiritually if you don't have a functioning family altar.

In today's world, parents are so distracted by the demands of life —work, bills, and societal pressures—that they forget the most important thing: their children's spiritual destiny. But if you neglect this, you are setting them up for failure and leaving them exposed to spiritual attacks. Without a family altar, your children are like sheep without a shepherd, easily led astray by the world.

The solution? Establish a family altar today. Pray over your children, sacrifice your time, and bring them into a deep, personal relationship with God. Please don't wait until it's too late. Look at Samson's life and learn from his parents' mistakes. Don't fail your children by neglecting the altar. In James 5:16 (KJV), the Bible says, "The effectual fervent prayer of a righteous man availed much." Let your prayers, sacrifices, and altar be the foundation upon which your children's destinies are built.

Do Not Be A Waste To God

You Must Value Altars

Break Down In Communication

When you read the scripture, it is evident that God had great plans for Samson, which could have made him one of the greatest leaders in Israel's history. Look at the prophecy upon his life again: Judges 13:3 (KJV): *"And the angel of the Lord appeared unto the woman and said unto her, Behold now, thou art barren, and bearest not; but thou shalt conceive, and bear a son."* This prophecy wasn't just a regular blessing; it was a divine assignment, and Samson was supposed to answer Israel's oppression by the Philistines. Yet, despite this extraordinary beginning, Samson's story ends in failure.

Why? Because Samson never valued the power of the altar in his life. He had God's favor, as a prophetic word was spoken over him even before he was born, yet he wasted it all. This is a clear warning to every Christian today that no matter how great your calling is, if you do not build and maintain an altar, you can still waste your life.

Every child of God has potential and a calling, but it is our responsibility to nurture it through a strong spiritual life powered by a functional altar. When you neglect this, you neglect the very foundation of your destiny. Samson had strength, favor, and opportunity, but he lacked one critical thing: "a connection to God through an active altar. "Without this, his strength became a tool for destruction rather than for divine purpose.

Today, we see so many people who have enormous potential;

they're talented, gifted, and full of promise, yet they live unfulfilled lives. Why? Because they have neglected their spiritual altars. They are more concerned with pursuing success in their careers, chasing after relationships, or accumulating material wealth than nurturing their connection with God. Just like Samson, they waste their divine potential because they fail to value the power of the altar. For example, think about someone who has a natural talent for leadership. They may rise quickly in their career, achieve worldly success, and gain influence, but without a solid spiritual foundation, that success will soon crumble. They will even face moral failure, burnout, and lack of peace because they have neglected the spiritual side of their lives. This is precisely what happened to Samson. He had all the external signs of success, strength, fame, and power, but internally, he was spiritually disconnected because there was no altar behind Him. His downfall wasn't sudden; it resulted from years of neglecting his altar.

Many families today are suffering because their parents have neglected their altars, so you see Children grow up in homes where there is no prayer, no sacrifice, and no spiritual instruction. As a result, these children are spiritually lost, much like Samson was. Proverbs 22:6 (KJV), which I quoted before, says, *"Train up a child in the way he should go: and when he is old, he will not depart from it."* But how can you train a child correctly if no altar exists in your home? Without a spiritual foundation, children are left vulnerable to the distractions and temptations of the world. This is a serious issue in today's society. There are too many children growing up with no sense of purpose, turning to drugs, violence, or unhealthy relationships because they don't have the spiritual guidance they need.

If you don't want to be a waste to God, you must prioritize your altar. It's not enough to be successful in the eyes of the world; true success comes from fulfilling your divine purpose. And that purpose can only be discovered and nurtured through a strong relationship with God, built on the foundation of a spiritual altar.

Break Down In Communication

Many of us are like Samson, carrying the weight of divine investment but doing nothing with it. Some of us are miserable right now because we know deep down that we are wasting the gifts and talents God gave us. Even though God has shown you that He is with you, even though He's put opportunities in your path, it's like pouring water into a basket with holes. All that divine investment is leaking away because there's no altar to hold it together. This was Samson's problem; he had a calling but no altar, no commitment to prayer, and no relationship with God.

Even more tragic is that Samson's parents weren't strangers to spiritual things. They understood the power of sacrifice and altar. His mother gave up her love for wine and strong drink because the angel of the Lord had told her not to consume these things for the sake of her son (Judges 13:7, KJV).

Why couldn't God ever talk directly to Samson, the man He had invested so much in? The Bible tells us that God had to use what Samson liked, his lusts, and desires to set him up for destiny. This is a sad commentary on Samson's life. Instead of God leading him through a direct relationship, He had to manipulate situations to get Samson to fulfill even a fraction of his purpose. Judges 14:4 (KJV) says, "But his father and his mother knew not that it was of the Lord, that he sought an occasion against the Philistines." Even in Samson's disobedience, God was still working, but how much more could have been accomplished if Samson had obeyed? How much more could he have done if he had valued the altar and sought God's guidance?

God should never have to set us up to fulfill our destinies. We should be so connected to Him that His will flows naturally through our lives. But when we neglect the altar and refuse to pray and seek Him, we force Him to use circumstances, trials, and sometimes even our mistakes to steer us back on course. This is not how it should be. God desires to speak to us directly and guide us lovingly, but that can only happen when we have an active, functioning altar.

Look around you, and you will see many people like Samson with incredible potential and prophetic words. God has invested heavily in their lives, but they are wasting it because they don't value their personal or family altar. They are distracted by the world, chasing after relationships, careers, and pleasures that pull them away from God. Like Samson, they are playing with fire, thinking their strength or talent will always be enough to get them out of trouble. But without an altar or spiritual connection to God, they are headed for disaster.

He had a supernatural birth, extraordinary strength, and a divine calling, yet his life ended in shame; his eyes were gouged out, he was chained, and he became a laughingstock to the very enemies he was supposed to defeat (Judges 16:21, KJV). When you neglect your spiritual life and your altar, you will end up blind, bound, and broken. It would be best if you did not let this happen to you. You must value the altar in your lives, not just because of yourself but for the sake of destiny and all who are connected to you, the fulfillment of your purpose. If you don't take care of your altar, you risk wasting everything God has invested in you. And make no mistake, God has invested much in you! He has given you talents, resources, opportunities, and, most importantly, His Spirit. But if you don't maintain your altar, all of that can be wasted.

The Force That Pulls

Consider this statement momentarily: "The force that pulls people down is always stronger than the force that pulls people up." When you think about it, you will realize that it is easier to fall in life than it is to rise. This is just another reason you cannot joke with your altar. You need a strong altar, a place of consistent prayer and sacrifice, to keep you connected to God and to protect you from the forces that seek to destroy your destiny. Proverbs 14:12 (KJV) says, *"There is a way which seemeth right unto a man, but the end thereof are the ways of death."* Samson thought he was strong enough to handle life on his terms, could play with sin, and still fulfill his purpose, but he was treading on sinking ground, and the same will happen to you if we neglect your altars.

The tragedy of Samson's life extends beyond his failure; it became a source of grief and disappointment for his parents as well. They had been given extraordinary insight into their son's life and calling before his birth, yet they watched helplessly as he rebelled against his purpose. Their failure to investigate and address Samson's rebellion points to a broader breakdown in spiritual leadership and the transmission of divine purpose from one generation to the next. No matter how positive or promising a prophecy or divine calling may be, if you do not take care to guard against tragedy and maintain an active altar life, you leave yourself vulnerable to failure because, as I said, the force that pulls people down is often stronger than the force that pulls up, making it imperative that we actively engage in spiritual disciplines that keep us connected to our divine source and strength who will pull us up in a way we cannot pull ourselves.

CHAPTER THREE

THE POWER OF
AN ALTAR TO
CAUSE CHANGE

Y ou hear me say things like, "My mother taught me to tithe; my mother taught me giving; my mother taught me sacrifices." If there is one thing I can tell you, my mother had a powerful altar at work. Her obedience to God and divine instructions were genuinely remarkable! Before I became saved, I laughed at her for doing a dry fast for three days for my salvation. Wow! She was indeed amazing! Can you imagine this woman fasting for three days with no food and no water, all because she wanted me saved? I even mockingly asked her, "Does God have to kill you to answer your prayer?" And she told me, "You will do the work of God and preach the word of God." I laughed and then left, but do you know what? Less than two weeks later, I was born again! Can you imagine that? That's the power of an altar!

Many things you are complaining about can drastically change when you master the power of an altar. Your financial challenges, marital challenges, the curses that hold you bound—I assure you they can all change. You need to become serious with your altar and the sacrifices on it. The power of an altar to cause change in our lives is rooted in its ability to connect us to God in a way that nothing else can do. Don't forget that we established that altars were gateways for supernatural interventions earlier. Your altar is also where you can lay down our burdens as your sacrifices rise to heaven. My mother understood this well, and she knew that her altar was a vital part of her spiritual life, and through her commitment, she was able to intercede for me.

When she fasted and prayed, she was not just going through the motions; she was invoking the power of God to intervene in my life, and each sacrifice she made was like fuel to the altar, igniting a divine response. This is the reality of an altar. It requires sacrifices to maintain its fire; when altars are neglected, their power diminishes, but when they are honored and tended to, I assure you they become mighty instruments of significant change. As I reflect on my mother's dedication, I can't help but think of the many who struggle with their altars. Many people despair over their situations, wondering why things never change. The answer often lies in their need for more engagement with their altars. If you want to see transformation in your life and break free from the chains that bind you, you must take your altar seriously.

Let me tell you something: the power of an altar can turn around your financial difficulties; there have been times when I thought I would not make it financially. But through prayer and the sacrifices I laid on my altar, things began to shift because God honors the commitments on the altar. He sees our dedication, and He responds in kind. So, when you face financial hardships, don't just complain; take it to your altar, make your sacrifices known to God, and watch as He opens doors and creates opportunities for you.

Let's talk about marital challenges because I know that relationships can be incredibly complex, and sometimes, it may even feel like you are fighting an uphill battle. However, the power of an altar can bring about healing and restoration. When I see couples struggling, I wish they would engage with their altars, pray, and make sacrifices; I assure you that it will cause wounds to heal and mend brokenness. It may not happen overnight, but the results will be astounding if both partners commit to working at their altar together.

This is not just a theoretical concept; altars are truly powerful. I have seen it happen repeatedly in my own life and the lives of others. My mother's altar was my anchor when I was at my lowest. Her faith and her sacrifices kept me grounded, and I believe that is what truly saved me, so child of God, you should know that the power of an altar is real and available to everyone. I want to challenge you today: how often do you engage with your altar? Are you making sacrifices? Are you praying fervently? Are you willing to put in the work to see change? Don't be like the many people today who find themselves in cycles of disappointment and wonder why nothing ever shifts. The answer lies in your altar. It is a spiritual tool that can be wielded to break through barriers and overcome obstacles.

Beloved, when you can master the power of an altar, you open the door to a new way of life. Your challenges diminish, your burdens become lighter, and the chains that once held you captive begin to break. It is not just about the big things but about the daily commitment to engage with God through your altar. Remember, the power of an altar is also about legacy. My mother's altar wasn't just for her but for me and generations to come. The sacrifices she made have a lasting impact on my life and the lives of even my children because I am also passing down the lessons I learned from her to them. You, too, can create a legacy through your altar, yes! Your decisions today will echo through time because you are setting a precedent for your children and their children.

In conclusion, I want to reiterate that the power of an altar to cause change is not just a concept; it is a reality you can experience in your life. You must be willing to engage, to sacrifice, and to believe. Don't let complacency hold you back. Embrace the power of your altar, and you will witness incredible transformations in your life. Remember, the fire of your altar can ignite change, and it all begins with you!

Pay You Price For Destiny

When You Are Making A Sacrifice For God, Be Serious About It

There are people who boldly claim they are giving up their jobs and everything else to devote themselves entirely to the work of God as a sacrifice, but when you take a closer examination, their actions reveal a different reality that they are not engaged in God's work at all. Instead, they are merely working for their own interests, looking for an excuse to avoid responsibilities or seeking personal gain under the guise of spiritual dedication. This is a troubling phenomenon that many do not recognize, yet it is crucial to address. You cannot tell me that you are sacrificing something for the sake of God's work while spending your mornings and afternoons at home, idly chatting on the phone or socializing with friends. If you genuinely offered a significant sacrifice for God's service, the evidence should be unmistakable in your actions and outcomes. The fruits of your labor should reflect your commitment. For instance, imagine if you truly gave up a stable job, and in two weeks, you managed to lead your entire street to Christ. That would be an undeniable testament to the impact of a true sacrifice for the Kingdom of God. Such an outcome exemplifies the kind of transformative power that comes from a sincere dedication to God's work.

Now, let us consider the scenario where you lose your job, regardless of the reasons behind that loss. If, in the weeks that follow, you find yourself simply playing around, avoiding meaningful engagement with your purpose, it raises significant questions about your true motivations. You once evangelized passionately and even faced repercussions for it to the point of losing your job because of your commitment to sharing the Gospel. But now, instead of continuing that mission, you have chosen to retreat into inactivity. Instead of going out and spreading the Good News, you are lounging around your home, spending countless hours scrolling through your phone or lost in a TV show. This behavior does not reflect a heart committed to God's service; it signifies a departure from the very calling you profess to hold dear.

Waiting and believing in God while remaining inactive and passive is not fulfilling the calling you claim to have. How can you expect to witness the power of God in your life if you are not actively pursuing the purpose He has set for you? God will not bestow the Holy Spirit or His divine power upon someone who is simply looking for entertainment or a leisurely existence. Such an attitude is tantamount to wasting precious time and resources. You cannot claim, "I spent all my time praying," if that prayer does not lead to action. Prayer should always inspire movement; it should compel you to seek answers and engage with the world around you.

Take, for example, Cornelius, He was a man of prayer and dedication, but he did not stop there, when God instructed him to send for Peter, Cornelius acted immediately, seeking out the very people who would guide him in fulfilling God's plan for his life. He understood that prayer without action is incomplete. The same principle applies to us today. If you assert that you are doing God's work, yet no one on your street is saved, I must ask you: who, then, is truly engaging in the work of God? Are you genuinely devoted to fulfilling His mission, or are you merely going through the motions?

God may have called you to start a business, and you might have made sacrifices for it, yet one critical aspect that often gets overlooked is the need to study and prepare for that business. You may sleep in, pretending that you are diligently working, but deep down, your destiny knows the truth that you are not engaging in any productive endeavors. This disconnect between intention and action is dangerous and counterproductive. When you are genuinely committed to your purpose, you should not need more than three months to begin making an impact because a true calling will compel you to be proactive, to seek out solutions, and to tackle challenges head-on. In truth, you will find yourself immersed in learning everything necessary to understand your call, reach out to bless others and explore innovative ways to serve the people God has called you to serve. What I am saying is "Your efforts should be characterized by a relentless pursuit of excellence and a dedication to your mission."

If in truth you become this committed to destiny why will God need to set you up so you can fulfill destiny? Why will he need to use your weaknesses to push you towards destiny? There will be no need! Take the example of Samson; he didn't need to be led astray by personal choices to fulfill God's purpose. Similarly, Gideon did not have to marry a Midianite to carry out God's will. If God must resort to using marriage or personal relationships to motivate people to engage in His work, it raises significant questions about the depth of their commitment. How many people will you marry, and how many divorces will arise from that before we all learn the lessons we need to learn?

The reality is that true sacrifice on your altar requires sincerity and dedication, when you make sacrifices for God, it is essential to take them seriously; do not deceive yourself into thinking that half-hearted efforts will suffice, no! God is seeking individuals who are fully committed, who are willing to pay the price, and who are dedicated to living out their calling with integrity and purpose. The work of God demands diligence, focus, and a willingness to step out of your comfort zone.

True sacrifices will always be evident; they cannot be hidden behind a veil of excuses or distractions so if you want to impact the world meaningfully, you need to get up, act, and start making a difference. You cannot afford to sit idly by and expect God to bless your efforts if you are not genuinely investing time and energy into fulfilling His purpose.

When you fully embrace the call to sacrifice for God, you position yourself as a vessel for His work, opening doors to blessings and opportunities that you may not have imagined possible because your altar is now functional. It is time to rise, shake off the distractions, and commit to the work of the Kingdom with every ounce of your being. Embrace the call, make your sacrifices count, and watch as God moves powerfully in your life and the lives of those around you.

CHAPTER FOUR

YOUR ALTAR IS WHAT SHOULD DRAW YOU INTO DESTINY

A functional altar is meant to serve as the foundation that draws you closer to your destiny, empowering you to fulfill the purpose that God has laid out for you. It is a place where your prayers, sacrifices, and commitments will align you with divine guidance, allowing you to walk confidently on the path that has been set before you. But then, when you do not heed the direction of your altar, when you are ignoring the call of destiny God may resort to using painful experiences, trials, and challenges to wake you up to the reality of your purpose. It is in these moments that divine intervention, though harsh, becomes necessary to correct your stubbornness and redirect your life toward your intended path.

Do you remember the events surrounding Samson's relationship with Delilah? This was not a relationship doomed by mere chance. In fact, it was a divine setup. On the night of Samson's wedding, Delilah betrayed him and betrayed the man who was gifted with incredible strength, a man who could single-handedly defeat a thousand enemies. The very first time Delilah faced pressure from the Philistines, she caved in without hesitation. She was married to the strongest man in the land, yet she feared these insignificant

Philistines. Her betrayal was not just a personal failure; it was the catalyst God used to set Samson on the painful journey he needed to fulfill his destiny because he had no functional altar through which God would direct his path.

This incident illustrates how God may allow pain into your life to capture your attention when you stubbornly resist His call. Often, the challenges and trials we face are not mere accidents, they are divine setups designed to shake us out of complacency. Samson, despite being divinely empowered, needed this betrayal to wake up to the reality of his destiny. And just like Samson, when you refuse to learn from the lessons of your altar, God will sometimes use your painful experiences and trials to push you in the right direction. But the question we should all ask ourselves is, how much pressure do you need to finally submit to God's will?

The answer to that should be simple: ZERO! You should need no pain, no sorrow, no tragedy to fall in line with God's purpose. Yet so many of us delay our destiny, forcing God's hand to use difficult circumstances to realign us with His plan. God has called you to a specific purpose, whether it be in business, ministry, politics, or something else, and instead of moving quickly and obediently, you are delaying. It may have taken you months, even years, to take the necessary steps toward that calling, what you do not know is that in this delay, you are beginning to establish a pattern of disobedience and a pattern of resistance, all of which are very dangerous. When I moved to the location where our church is now located, I did not wait to start a church. I did not sit idle, waiting for the perfect conditions. Rather, in my small apartment, I started a church because I understood the urgency of responding to God's call. I also knew that delay breeds disobedience, and I was determined not to let that happen.

The point here is simple, what is your calling and purpose? What has God called you to do? Do you have an altar, a place where you can commune with God and gain clarity on your destiny? You may even say yes, but if your altar is not pulling you into your purpose, then something is wrong. Your altar should empower you, not paralyze you and it should bring you closer to your destiny, not away from it.

Altar and Spiritual Dynamics at Work

It was easy not to realize that God was using Delilah's betrayal as a setup for Samson to eventually destroy the Philistines, everyone thought it was just another tragic incident in the man's life, but in reality, it was a divine orchestration to push Samson into his ultimate purpose of confronting and eventually destroying the Philistines. Sometimes, we do not recognize the pain we experience as part of God's greater plan for us, but if you maintain a functional altar, one that is consistently in line with God's will, you will not need these painful setups. Instead, your altar will guide you naturally toward your destiny without the need for tragedy or hardship.

Your altar should serve as a place of divine fire, a place where God's presence is so strong that if, for any reason, you begin to drift away from His purpose, your altar will realign your life, it will reignite the passion, and it will bring back the focus you need for the fulfillment of your destiny thereby eliminating the need for painful experiences to get you back on track.

The goal here is to eliminate tragedy and restore dignity and glory in your walk with God. Your altar should be a source of strength, not a place of weakness or confusion. If you maintain a strong, consistent altar, you can pursue and fulfill your destiny without unnecessary sorrow or hardship; this is God's glorious intention for you.

Take Delilah as an example of how easily betrayal can happen when you are not aligned with your destiny, Delilah gave in to pressure and betrayed Samson for a sum of money. The tragedy here is that she could not even see the bigger picture. She was married to a man who had the strength and anointing to protect her and her family. Samson had the power to kill a thousand men single-handedly, and yet, Delilah feared the threats of a few Philistines. She could not see beyond the immediate pressure and, in her short-sightedness, did not realize that being with Samson's destiny would have brought her far greater rewards than whatever the Philistines had to offer.

Onetime, Samson presented a riddle to the Philistines during his wedding feast, recorded in Judges 14:12-14 he said *"Let me now put forth a riddle to you. If you can give me the correct answer within the seven days of the feast, I will give you thirty linen garments and thirty changes of clothes. But if you cannot tell me the answer, then you shall give me thirty linen garments and thirty changes of clothes."* The riddle was *"Out of the eater, something to eat; out of the strong, something sweet."* The Philistines where unable to solve the riddle so they threatened Delilah, pressuring her to get the answer from Samson. If Delilah had thought about the situation clearly, she would have realized that the Philistines' threats were empty in the face of Samson's strength. If they failed to solve the riddle, they would have had to pay Samson, making both wealthy. Instead of betraying her husband-to-be, she could have supported him, trusting that he would protect her and her family from any danger. But she didn't. She gave in to the pressure from the Philistines and continually pressed Samson until he revealed the answer, which she then passed on to the Philistines (Judges 14:15-17).

What I need you to see right now is that everything looked physical, but several spiritual dynamics were at work. First of all, the Altar of the Philistines were making Delilah foolish, and secondly, Samson's lack of a fervent altar was the reason he kept falling into danger on the laps of Delilah like a fool. But God was also planning to use the whole situation to His advantage because since Samson was being foolish and had refused to take his altar seriously, the Lord knew he would have to use this terrible situation to help Samson in fulfilling the destiny of destroying the Philistines at the end.

As a result of her betrayal, regarding the riddle Samson had given to her people, Samson was forced into a difficult situation, He had to use his God-given strength not to build or protect, but to fight and kill to fulfill a meaningless demand. Samson, in response to their deceit, went down to Ashkelon and killed thirty men to take their clothes and give them to those who had "solved" the riddle through Delilah's deception (Judges 14:19). This tragic turn of events could have been avoided if Delilah had understood the true power and purpose of Samson's anointing. Instead, she set him on a path filled with unnecessary pain and conflict.

Indeed, the story of Samson and Delilah serves as a powerful reminder that when we do not align ourselves with God's purpose, we invite unnecessary pain and tragedy into our lives. This is why understanding the true nature of our calling is crucial, as it not only protects us from harm but also allows us to walk in the full strength of God's provision (Proverbs 3:5-6).

True Value! Valu!! Value!!!

Don't Value People of Wrong Altars or No Altars More Than You Value God's Prophets, And the Altars of Your Life

You should know that the people you choose to surround yourself with and the altars that you allow to influence you are of immense importance. Your connection to God, the altar you establish with Him, and the people who uphold similar values should always take precedence in your life. Too often, people make the mistake of valuing relationships with individuals who do not have a godly altar or no altar at all. They place more trust in these relationships than they do in their connection with God or in the men and women who speak into their lives through prophetic insight and godly altars. This misplaced trust can lead you astray, as those without a foundation in God can unconsciously, or even consciously, steer you off the path of righteousness. Do not forget, the bible lets us know that evil company can corrupt good manners, this means that the influence of those who have no godly altar can severely undermine your spiritual foundation.

Some even value the opinions and influence of parents or close family members, over the word of a prophet. This is not to say that you should not respect or love your parents, but if they are not rooted in God and are not attuned to the altar that you are building, their advice can sometimes be misguided. It's a dangerous thing to trust those who do not have the spiritual foundation necessary to guide you toward God's destiny for your life. Your respect for your spouse or family member should not outweigh your reverence for the altar that backs your life, especially if they are not aligned with the will of God.

When it comes to valuing people in your life, you must be discerning, there are those who, while close to you, may manipulate or mislead you, intentionally or unintentionally just like Delilah did to Samson, this is to say that you must always ask yourself whether the people around you value the altar you have built with God. If they do not, then their presence in your life can become detrimental to your destiny. Samson trusted Delilah, a woman who had no regard for God or for Samson's divine purpose, at the end Her manipulation led to his downfall. Had Samson placed more trust in the prophetic voice of God, or in his own spiritual convictions, rather than in the manipulations of Delilah, his story could have been different. The lesson here is simple, value the people who honor God and the altars they build, and be wary of those who do not, no matter how close or beloved they may be.

Rebellion against those who contradict your altar

If you find that there are manipulative forces or people trying to infiltrate your altar, trying to steer you away from your divine calling, it is your responsibility to flush them out. There is no room for manipulation when it comes to the things of God. Your altar should be a place of purity, free from the influence of deceitful voices and you must rebel against these contradictions, making it clear that your life and your destiny are not up for manipulation by forces or people who do not walk in line with God's will.

Let it be that whenever you are close to falling into a satanic trap, something will intervene, whether it be divine protection or a clear exposure of your adversaries. God can and will expose the intentions of those who seek to harm you, but only if you are diligent in maintaining a strong altar and not allowing those with no godly foundation to influence your life.

Imagine what could have happened if the women who led Solomon into idolatry had never entered his life, or if their manipulation had been exposed before they could turn him away from God. Solomon, the wisest man who ever lived, found himself worshipping false gods because of the influence of the women in his life. These women tortured his spirit, and despite his wisdom, Solomon struggled against the forces of manipulation that they brought into his life. He fought against the demonic forces that these women introduced into his household, but in the end, their influence caused him to stray from his divine calling. Had these women been removed from his life earlier, or had Solomon been more discerning about the altars they worshipped, he might have avoided the spiritual downfall that followed.

Even the strongest and most anointed people are vulnerable to manipulation when they allow the wrong people into their lives. Solomon fought demons, locked them in the abyss, and dealt with the representatives of evil spirits, but the one thing he could not overcome was the emotional manipulation that these women brought into his life. What if, instead of falling prey to their influence, Solomon had been protected by divine intervention? What if the Angel of God had appeared to these women every night, warning them to leave Solomon alone? Perhaps then, like Moses' wife, they would have fled, leaving Solomon free to continue his walk with God without interference.

Speaking of Moses, he too faced manipulation from those close to him, his wife, at one point, prevented him from circumcising their sons, an act that was critical to fulfilling his divine duty. Moses had a weakness, and his desire to keep his marriage intact was that weakness, it caused him to momentarily fail in his calling because he allowed the manipulation to prevent him from doing what was right in the eyes of God. Eventually, his wife left him, calling him a "bloody husband" and leaving him with the boys. It was only after she left that Moses was able to fully walk in his purpose, and we see later in Scripture that his sons went on to serve as priests, fulfilling their own divine destinies. You see, when manipulation tries to interfere with your altar and your calling, it must be removed, no matter how difficult the separation may be.

This principle extends beyond personal relationships into other aspects of life, including your career. You may feel the temptation to quit your job, thinking that by doing so, you are freeing yourself to pursue your destiny, but it is important to remember that God values excellence in all areas of life, quitting a job prematurely, without a clear plan or divine direction, may not be the best course of action so you must learn to balance your responsibilities. "While you are servicing your job, you should also be servicing your destiny." Excellence in your work is not separate from your spiritual life, it is an extension of it so as you work, do so with the intention of glorifying God and fulfilling the purpose He has for you.

It is also important to understand that fatigue and exhaustion are sometimes part of the process. If you are tired, let it be for a season. Sacrifice is part of walking in your purpose, and sometimes that means working hard even when you are physically drained. However, ensure that you are still making progress toward the promise that God has for you. If you are diligent, the time will come when your side business or calling will grow to the point where you no longer need your job. At that point, you will be able to focus entirely on the destiny that God has laid out for you. But until then, do not despise the work that is in front of you. It is part of the journey out of the pit and into the purpose that God has for you.

Altar Intelligence

Programming Your Altars

Altar intelligence is something that most people are unaware of, yet it operates in their lives constantly, affecting their outcomes and decisions. It is akin to a form of artificial intelligence, an invisible but active force programmed by the individual through their spiritual actions and beliefs. Many times, people experience the repercussions of an altar working in their lives, whether for good or evil without realizing that it is the altar at work. They often believe that certain events or outcomes are simply "natural or luck" but the truth is that altar intelligence is at play, ensuring that the person either stays protected or faces consequences based on the programming they have established with their altar. This is why one must never take their altar before God lightly or ignore its significance.

Do you know that a door that seems like an opportunity can sometimes be a trap? Such a door can get shut by your altar to prevent you from walking into danger and you may even end up complaining feeling like you have missed an opportunity. Meanwhile, another door, one that leads to your true destiny can open for you and you may be feeling it is a bad door. This kind of divine intervention is often the result of altar intelligence. The more you invest in your altar, the stronger and more intelligent it becomes in guiding you and protecting you. Just like artificial intelligence becomes more refined the more it is used and trained, your altar grows in power and understanding the more you service it through prayer, sacrifice, and obedience to God.

When you think of altar intelligence, think of it as the intelligence that you infuse into it. Artificial intelligence only has the intelligence that we humans give to it. What this means is that your life of prayer, your sacrifices, and the intentional focus you put on your altar all contribute to its effectiveness and intelligence. If you program your altar with laziness, neglect, or indifference, it will reflect that. But if you feed it with the right kind of input, consistent prayer, sacrifice, worship, and a commitment to holiness your altar becomes a powerful force in your life, capable of warding off sabotage, manipulation, and evil intentions. Every time you pray, "I cast out every spirit of sabotage in my life," your altar hears that message and begins to act according to that programming. It now knows that you do not want sabotage in your life, and it goes to work, casting out any elements that may lead to your downfall.

The act of placing a sacrifice on your altar does more than just make you feel good or appear religious. It has a real and lasting effect on the spiritual intelligence of your altar. Sacrifices of time, praise, prayer, money, and obedience infuse life into your altar and when you consistently offer sacrifices to God, you are affirming your position as the owner and priest of that altar, so it can begin to operate with greater strength and effectiveness. A well-maintained altar is constantly working on your behalf, even when you are unaware of it. It is always flagging potential dangers and blocking tragedies before they can even reach you. For instance, if tragedy is coming your way, your altar, based on the intelligence it has gathered from your prayers and sacrifices will stand guard and prevent it from manifesting in your life. It is like having a spiritual firewall that protects you from attacks and threats you may not even see coming.

Imagine a scenario where your child has not prayed, but because you have an active, intelligent altar, it tracks your child and protects them from harm. Or imagine entering a vehicle where the driver has sinister intentions, planning to harm or even kill someone, but because your altar is active, it declares, "No weapon formed against me shall prosper." In these moments, your altar is functioning as a protective force, ensuring that no harm comes to you, even when you are not aware of the danger. This is the kind of intelligence that a well-maintained altar provides—it sees what you cannot see and acts in ways you may never fully understand.

Sometimes, the events that seem like tragedies in your life are divine interventions meant to save you from something far worse. You may cry over the loss of a friend, not realizing that this friend was secretly plotting your downfall. You may mourn the end of a relationship, unaware that this relationship was dragging you away from your divine purpose. This is the intelligence of your altar at work, acting on your behalf in ways that may not make sense to you in the moment but are for your good.

Look at the story of Samson. God used a woman, Delilah, to get Samson's attention, but Samson failed to recognize the warnings. His altar was intelligent enough to protect him, but he ignored the signs. The result was that the same people who pressured Delilah into betraying Samson burned her and her father's house to the ground. When you set up a great person to save yourself, as Delilah did, you may end up becoming the sacrifice yourself. The intelligence of Samson's altar was designed to protect him from such manipulations, but Samson's own weakness and the patterns he established with his altar worked against him. Instead of standing firm and rejecting Delilah's advances, Samson allowed his altar to be polluted by sending the wrong messages.

Careful The Decisions You Make

If you continually send the wrong signals to your altar through disobedience, sin, or spiritual laziness, it will reflect those signals in your life because your altar reflects the intelligence you put into it. If you fill it with sacrifice, obedience, and dedication to God, it will work tirelessly to protect and guide you. But if you neglect it and allow sin to fester, or continually make poor decisions, your altar will be weakened, and its ability to protect you will be diminished. This is why it is so critical to be intentional about the messages you send to your altar. Don't let weakness dominate your calling, as Samson did. Instead, stand firm, refuse to give in to manipulation, and let your altar work for you as it was designed to do.

Imagine having a powerful that keeps making the necessary sacrifices, and seeing your life transformed as a result? Your friends may laugh at you for being so committed to your altar, for making sacrifices of time, money, and obedience, but in the end, it is your altar that will stand strong when theirs falters. Just as you pay rent to live in a landlord's building, God expects you to offer your first fruits to live on His earth. When you do this, you signal to both God and your altar that you are serious about your commitment to His will.

There are countless stories of people being spared from tragedy because their altars intervened. Take, for example, the story of a funeral where a man killed 17 people in attendance. What if one of those 17 people had gone late, or their tire had been punctured, causing them to miss the tragedy? This is the intelligence of the altar at work. When you are connected to a powerful altar, it can twist circumstances, prevent harm, and ensure that you remain on the path to your destiny. God should be able to talk to you through your altar, guiding you away from tragedy and toward the fulfillment of His purpose for your life.

CHAPTER FIVE

5 ESSENTIALS YOU MUST TAKE NOTE OF

Every effort in life should be purposeful, intentional, and focused on the things that truly matter. In the realm of the sprit and spiritual growth, these efforts are especially important because they influence not only your present but also your future, your relationships, and even your eternal destiny. It is easy to become distracted by the multitude of demands and desires in life, but your efforts must be targeted at five key things to ensure that you are walking in alignment with God's will and purpose for your life.

1.   Build An Unshakable Relationship with God, No Matter the Cost

First, and most important, every effort of yours must be directed toward building a strong, stable, and functional relationship with God. This cannot be done half-heartedly or on a whim; it requires dedication, patience, and sacrifice. It does not matter how long it takes or how much it costs; you must be willing to invest everything into nurturing this relationship. There will be times when it feels like progress is slow or non-existent, but that is no reason to give up. The foundation of your life, your success, and your peace rests on how deep and solid your relationship with God is. Just like building a strong house takes time, effort, and high-quality materials, building a relationship with God requires similar dedication. You cannot rush the process, and you cannot shortcut the costs. You must be willing to engage in consistent prayer, studying of the Word, and a commitment to living in obedience to God's will.

2. Align with God's Purpose While Embracing Life's Blessings

While focusing on this relationship, it is also essential to aim your efforts toward finding and connecting with God's original purpose for your life. So many people get lost in the day-to-day pursuits mundane things without ever pausing to ask, "What was I really created to do?" These things, your job, marriage, and business are important, but they are secondary to the larger question of your purpose. There is an original plan for your life, something unique that only you can fulfill. When you find that purpose and connect with it, everything else begins to fall into place. It is like finding the key to a lock that has been stubbornly refusing to open. Once you are in with God's original plan for your life, all the secondary pursuits, such as your career, marriage, or academics, become more meaningful and fruitful. You enjoy the benefits of these aspects of your life, but they no longer consume or define you. Instead,

Instead, these secondary pursuits become tools and platforms for you to express and fulfill God's purpose for your life. Your job, your marriage, and your business are no longer about making a living or finding personal satisfaction; they become avenues through which you live out the original plan God has for you. This shift in focus brings clarity, peace, and a sense of divine direction. You are no longer chasing after fleeting successes or temporary satisfactions but are firmly grounded in the eternal purpose for which you were created.

3. Sanctify And Strengthen The Altars That Shape Your Life

The third area where your efforts must be concentrated is in structuring, restructuring, sanctifying, and satisfying the altars that govern your life. Whether you realize it or not, everyone's life is governed by altars. An altar represents a place of divine exchange, where covenants are made, and where spiritual authority is exercised. It can be a place of blessing or a place of bondage, depending on how it is maintained and serviced. This is why Elijah, before calling down fire from heaven, first repaired the broken altar. If the altar servicing your life is broken, polluted, or neglected, it will send the wrong message to the spiritual realm. A broken altar is one that has been contaminated by sin, false beliefs, or neglect. It is an altar that no longer commands the attention of heaven, one that no longer connects you to the source of divine power.

Your efforts must be aimed at ensuring that your altar is not only intact but also fully functional. This means daily sacrifices of prayer, worship, and obedience. It means removing any form of pollution, whether it comes from relationships, behaviors, or beliefs that are not in alignment with God's will. If you have entered a covenant with the wrong people or allowed sinful habits to pollute your life, you must take deliberate steps to cleanse your altar. Every time you sense that something has gone wrong spiritually—whether it is a loss of peace, a pattern of failure, or a spiritual heaviness—you must immediately address it. Do not allow contamination to fester. The moment you notice it, act to remove it and restore the sanctity of your altar.

It is also important to understand that your altar receives and responds to the intelligence you send to it. If you engage in behaviors or relationships that are contrary to God's design, your altar gets the message that these things are acceptable, and it adjusts accordingly. For example, if you enter a relationship with someone who is spiritually compromised, you are sending a message to your altar that you are okay with that level of spiritual contamination. This can weaken your altar and make you vulnerable to spiritual attacks. On the other hand, when you dedicate yourself to purity and sanctification, your altar becomes a strong, fortified place of divine protection and blessing. Your efforts must be constant in making sure that your altar is not only structured and restructured but also continually sanctified and satisfied with the right kind of sacrifices—sacrifices of praise, prayer, and obedience.

4. Pursue Divine Restoration of Your Lost or Weakened Glory

The fourth area that requires your targeted effort is the restoration of lost or weakened glory. Throughout life, you will experience seasons where it feels like the brightness of your life has dimmed, or where you have lost something vital—whether it is a sense of purpose, favor, or even opportunities. In these moments, you must not give in to despair but instead, make every effort to pray for and expect divine restoration. Restoration is a promise from God, but it requires your cooperation. You must actively look out for divine signs of restoration in your life. These signs may not always be grand or immediately recognizable, but they are there. For instance, it may be something as small as a renewed passion for prayer or a reconnection with someone who plays a key role in your destiny.

Many people miss their moment of restoration because they are too focused on what they have lost or are distracted by trivial things. If you find yourself awake at night, do not waste that time on social media or watching TV. God is waking you up to pray, to engage with Him in the quiet hours where distractions are few. If you sense even the smallest shift in your life, whether it is someone giving you an encouraging word, an unexpected opportunity, or simply a renewed sense of hope, celebrate that. These are signs that God is restoring you, piece by piece, moment by moment.

Restoration is often a process, not an event. Just as Samson's hair began to grow back slowly after he had lost his strength, so too will the glory of your life begin to return little by little. You may not see the full picture right away, but every step of restoration is significant. Pay attention to the little victories, the small signs of favor, and the moments of grace that come your way. These are evidence that God is working behind the scenes, restoring what has been lost or weakened. Keep your eyes open for these divine signs and make sure to respond in faith and gratitude.

5. Seize Every Divine Opportunity in All You Do

Finally, every effort of yours must be aimed at taking advantage of divine opportunities. Life is full of opportunities, but not all of them are from God. It requires discernment and spiritual sensitivity to recognize the divine opportunities that are aligned with your purpose. When these opportunities arise, you must seize them with both hands, making the most of every open door that God gives you. Like Samson placing his hands on the pillars of the Philistine temple, you must be strategic and intentional in how you use the opportunities God provides.

But there is an important warning here, do not let the problem you were born to solve become the thing that kills you. Samson was born to defeat the Philistines, but he allowed his own weaknesses to lead him to a place where the very people ultimately killed him he was destined to defeat. This is a cautionary tale for all of us. You must put in the effort to overcome your personal weaknesses and flaws, so that they do not sabotage the very mission God has called you to fulfill. Whether it is a lack of discipline, a tendency toward complacency, or a vulnerability to temptation, you must find and address these areas with the help of God's grace and wisdom. Your altar will also play a crucial role in this. As you put in the effort to sanctify and strengthen your altar, it will become a place of divine intelligence that guides and protects you. It will help you navigate life's challenges, steering you away from pitfalls and keeping you focused on your mission. An altar that is properly serviced and maintained will not allow you to be defeated by the very thing you were born to overcome. It will act as a spiritual shield, ensuring that you fulfill your destiny without being destroyed in the process.

Every effort you make must be deliberate and targeted toward these five key areas which are building a strong relationship with God, connecting with His original purpose for your life, structuring and sanctifying your altar, praying for the restoration of lost glory, and seizing divine opportunities. When you focus your efforts in these areas, you will find that your life becomes more in line with God's will, and you will experience His favor, protection, and guidance in everything you do. It won't always be easy, and the road may be long, but the rewards are eternal, and the fulfillment of living out your divine purpose is worth every sacrifice you make.

CHAPTER SIX

PRAYER ON YOUR ALTAR & RELEASING SPIRITUAL POWER

Releasing Fiery Prayers

Many people think prayer is about communication with God, but you see, prayer is beyond that. Prayer is how you do business in the Spirit; it is about leaving the natural realm and dealing with the supernatural realm. An altar without sacrifices is not an altar, what makes an altar potent is that there are sacrifices upon it. When God was speaking to the Priest, He said, the fire on the altar must not go out, and the Bible tells us in the book of Peter that we are meant to offer up spiritual sacrifices. Let me be straight and plain here, "Prayer is one of the greatest sacrifices you must learn to offer on your Spiritual Altar" I am not talking about a wishy-washy kind of prayer, where you just pray absent-mindedly as though God is forcing you to call upon His name.

What I am talking about is a Prayer that consumes your soul, your body, and your spirit. This is not a prayer you pray underneath your breath; it is a burning and fervent level of Supplication. Prayer is not just a casual activity; true prayer is how you engage the spirit realm. Other things may be theoretical, but prayer is a verb, and when you truly engage in fiery prayers such as this, tremendous power is released. Angels are mobilized, and your spirit becomes hypersensitive to the realm of the Spirit. This is the level where you give commands, and demons flee. You give commands, and situations change because the incense of prayer on your altar is ascending to God as a sweet-smelling savor and living sacrifice.

The Apostle Paul, understanding the power of such fervent prayer, exhorted the church in Thessalonica, saying, "Pray without ceasing" (1 Thessalonians 5:17, KJV). This was not a mere suggestion but a command, recognizing that constant communion with God through prayer is the lifeline of our spiritual existence. It's through this unceasing prayer that we maintain a vibrant and active altar before the Lord.

Think about the example of Elijah on Mount Carmel, the Bible tells us in 1 Kings 18:36-38 (KJV), *"And it came to pass at the time of the offering of the evening sacrifice, that Elijah the prophet came near, and said, LORD God of Abraham, Isaac, and of Israel, let it be known this day that thou art God in Israel, and that I am thy servant, and that I have done all these things at thy word. Hear me, O LORD, hear me, that this people may know that thou art the LORD God, and that thou hast turned their heart back again. Then the fire of the LORD fell, and consumed the burnt sacrifice, and the wood, and the stones, and the dust, and licked up the water that was in the trench."* This powerful demonstration of God's response to fervent prayer shows us the potency of a well-maintained spiritual altar.

The power released through prayer is not just about personal edification, but it has far-reaching effects in the spiritual realm. When we engage in fiery prayers, we are not just speaking words into the air; we are wielding spiritual weapons that have divine power to demolish strongholds. The Bible says 2 Corinthians 10:4 (KJV), "For the weapons of our warfare are not carnal, but mighty through God to the pulling down of strong holds."

I tell you the truth, the power of prayer on your altar is not limited by time or space because through prayer, you can affect situations and circumstances far beyond your physical reach and this is beautifully illustrated in the story of Peter's imprisonment in Acts 12. While Peter was in prison, the church was fervently praying for him. What was the result? An angel was dispatched to miraculously free Peter from his chains and lead him out of the prison. This demonstrates that when we pray, we are not limited by physical barriers; our prayers can penetrate prison walls and break chains.

6 Practical Steps To Building An Effective And Constant Prayer Life That Will Always Set Fire On Your Altar And Release God's Power

- **Choose a specific space or room and consecrate it as your meeting place with God:**

The first step in building an effective and constant prayer life is to establish a dedicated prayer space. This is not about creating a fancy prayer room, but rather about setting apart a specific area where you can consistently meet with God. This could be a corner of your bedroom, a quiet spot in your living room, or even a particular chair where you sit to pray. The key is consistency. When you choose this space, take time to consecrate it unto the Lord. This act of consecration is not about the physical space itself, but about your heart's commitment to make this a holy meeting place between you and God. You might anoint the area with oil, as we see in Genesis 28:18 (KJV) where Jacob "took the stone that he had put for his pillows, and set it up for a pillar, and poured oil upon the top of it." This act symbolizes setting apart this space for God's purposes.

Remember, the power of this space does not lie in its physical attributes, but in your faithful use of it for prayer. As you consistently meet God in this place, it will become saturated with His presence. Over time, merely entering this space will begin to stir your spirit towards prayer.

- **Choose A specific Time and keep to it:**

Consistency is key in building a powerful prayer life. Just as you have chosen a specific place, now choose a specific time for prayer, and stick to it religiously. This discipline is crucial in developing a prayer life that sets fire on your altar and releases God's power. The Bible gives us many examples of people who had set times for prayer. Daniel, for instance, prayed three times a day at set times, even when it put his life at risk (Daniel 6:10, KJV). David declared in Psalm 55:17 (KJV), "Evening, and morning, and at noon, will I pray, and cry aloud: and he shall hear my voice." When choosing your prayer time, consider when you are most alert and least likely to be interrupted. For many, early morning works best, following the example of Jesus who often rose early to pray (Mark 1:35, KJV). Others might find late evening more suitable. The exact time is not as important as your consistency in keeping it.

- **Prepare your heart and mind before entering your prayer time:**

Before you enter your designated prayer space at your set time, take a few moments to prepare your heart and mind. This preparation is crucial in transitioning from the busyness of life to a focused time of communion with God. Start by quieting your thoughts and centering your mind on God. You might want to meditate on a Scripture verse or simply sit in silence, acknowledging God's presence. The Psalmist models this in Psalm 46:10 (KJV), which says, "Be still, and know that I am God."

Part of this preparation should also involve examining your heart. The Bible tells us in Psalm 66:18 (KJV), "If I regard iniquity in my heart, the Lord will not hear me." Take time to confess any sins and ask for forgiveness, ensuring that nothing hinders your communion with God.

- **Structure your prayer time:**

Although spontaneity in prayer is beautiful, having a structure can also help you maintain focus and ensure you cover all aspects of prayer. A helpful model is the ACTS prayer structure:

Adoration: Begin by praising God for who He is. This aligns your heart with His greatness and sets the tone for your prayer time.

Confession: Acknowledge your sins and shortcomings to God, accepting His forgiveness.

Thanksgiving: Express gratitude for God's blessings and answered prayers.

Supplication: Bring your requests to God, for yourself and others.

This structure reflects the pattern Jesus gave in the Lord's Prayer (Matthew 6:9-13, KJV), which begins with adoration ("Hallowed be thy name"), includes submission to God's will, requests for provision and forgiveness, and ends with an acknowledgment of God's power and glory.

- **Incorporate Scripture into your prayer:**

Praying Scripture is a powerful way to align your prayers with God's will and to fuel the fire on your prayer altar. As you read the Bible, let it inspire and guide your prayers. When you pray God's words back to Him, you are declaring His truth and promises over your life and situations.

For instance, if you are praying for strength, you might pray Philippians 4:13 (KJV): "Lord, Your Word says I can do all things through Christ which strengtheneth me. I claim this promise today as I face my challenges."

Praying Scripture also helps when you don't know what to pray. Romans 8:26 (KJV) reminds us that "the Spirit also helpeth our infirmities: for we know not what we should pray for as we ought: but the Spirit itself maketh intercession for us with groanings which cannot be uttered."

· Cultivate an attitude of expectancy:

Approach your prayer time with faith and expectancy, believing that God hears and will answer. Jesus emphasized the importance of faith in prayer, saying in Mark 11:24 (KJV), "Therefore I say unto you, what things soever ye desire, when ye pray, believe that ye receive them, and ye shall have them." This does not mean that God will always answer in the way or timing we expect, but it does mean we can trust that He hears and responds according to His perfect will. Cultivating this attitude of expectancy keeps the fire burning on your prayer altar, even when answers seem delayed.

Implementing these six steps consistently will transform your prayer life from a mere religious duty into a powerful, life-changing encounter with the living God. Remember, building such a prayer life takes time and persistence. There will be days when you do not want to pray or when distractions seem overwhelming. In those moments, remind yourself of the words of Galatians 6:9 (KJV): "And let us not be weary in well doing: for in due season we shall reap, if we faint not." As you faithfully maintain your prayer altar through these practices, you'll find that your spiritual sensitivity increases, your relationship with God deepens, and you begin to see His power released in unprecedented ways in your life and circumstances. Your prayer life will become not just a part of your day, but the very foundation upon which your day is built.

Also, as you consistently engage in this kind of focused, intentional prayer, you will find that prayer begins to permeate every aspect of your life. You will start to develop what the Apostle Paul called praying "without ceasing" (1 Thessalonians 5:17, KJV). This does not mean you are constantly in a posture of formal prayer, but rather that your entire life becomes a conversation with God, where you are constantly aware of His presence and in tune with His Spirit.

Do not forget, the goal of all these practices is not to create a rigid, legalistic prayer routine, but to cultivate a vibrant, living relationship with God. As you faithfully tend to your prayer altar through these steps, you will find it becoming a place of tremendous spiritual power, a place where heaven and earth meet, and where God's power is released into your life and the world around you.

7 Hindrances To The Kind Of Prayer That Released Tremendous Power From Your Altar

Inconsistency:

Do not treat your prayer life and prayer time with levity. In fact, any attack that can affect your prayer life is a real attack from the enemy and can-do great damage to you. Inconsistency in prayer is like trying to light a fire with wet wood; it sputters and dies out before it can really catch. The power released from your prayer altar is directly proportional to the consistency with which you tend it. The Bible emphasizes the importance of persistence in prayer. In Luke 18:1 (KJV), Jesus told a parable "To this end, that men ought always to pray, and not to faint." This parable of the persistent widow demonstrates that consistency in prayer is not just about fulfilling a religious duty, but about persevering until we see results.

Inconsistency in prayer can stem from various sources like busyness, lack of discipline, or simply forgetting. To combat this, we must make prayer a non-negotiable priority in our lives. Just as we would not skip meals because we are too busy, we should not neglect our spiritual nourishment through prayer. The enemy knows the power of consistent prayer, and he will do everything he can to disrupt your prayer life. Be on guard against his tactics. As Peter warns us in 1 Peter 5:8 (KJV), "Be sober, be vigilant; because your adversary the devil, as a roaring lion, walketh about, seeking whom he may devour."

Sin:

Sin is the most significant hindrance to powerful prayer. It creates a barrier between us and God, muffling our prayers and dampening the fire on our altar. The prophet Isaiah clearly said this truth: "But your iniquities have separated between you and your God, and your sins have hid his face from you, that he will not hear" (Isaiah 59:2, KJV). This does not mean that we must be perfect to pray effectively, but it does mean that we need to approach God with a repentant heart, confessing our sins and seeking His forgiveness. The Psalmist understood this when he wrote, "If I regard iniquity in my heart, the Lord will not hear me" (Psalm 66:18, KJV).

Sin not only hinders our prayers but also dulls our spiritual senses, making us less sensitive to God's voice and leading. It is like trying to tune into a radio station with a lot of static interference; the signal (God's voice) is still there, but our sin makes it difficult to hear clearly. To maintain a powerful prayer altar, we must regularly examine our hearts, confess our sins, and seek God's cleansing. As John assures us, "If we confess our sins, he is faithful and just to forgive us our sins, and to cleanse us from all unrighteousness" (1 John 1:9, KJV).

Associating With Demonic Altars:

You cannot mix God and the devil together; light and darkness have nothing in common, and your life cannot change that, so if you try to maintain a powerful prayer altar while also dabbling in practices associated with demonic altars is not only ineffective but dangerous. The bible makes this clear by saying "Ye cannot drink the cup of the Lord, and the cup of devils: ye cannot be partakers of the Lord's table, and of the table of devils" (1 Corinthians 10:21, KJV). Any association with demonic altars - be it through occult practices, idolatry, or even harboring bitterness and unforgiveness - can severely hinder the power of your prayers. This principle extends beyond obvious occult practices. Sometimes, we unknowingly give place to demonic influence through the media we consume, the relationships we maintain, or the thoughts we entertain. Paul advises us to be vigilant: "Neither give place to the devil" (Ephesians 4:27, KJV). To maintain a powerful prayer altar, we must be diligent in guarding our hearts and minds against any demonic influence.

Lack of Faith:

Faith is the currency of the spiritual realm, and without it, our prayers lack power. The author of Hebrews states unequivocally, "But without faith it is impossible to please him: for he that cometh to God must believe that he is, and that he is a rewarder of them that diligently seek him" (Hebrews 11:6, KJV). When we pray without faith, we are like the waves of the sea, driven and tossed by the wind, as James describes, "But let him ask in faith, nothing wavering. For he that wavereth is like a wave of the sea driven with the wind and tossed. For let not that man think that he shall receive any thing of the Lord" (James 1:6-7, KJV).

You see, lack of faith can manifest in various ways such as praying without expecting an answer, doubting God's willingness or ability to intervene, or simply going through the motions of prayer without really believing in its power. To combat this, we must constantly feed our faith through the Word of God, testimonies of answered prayers, and reflecting on God's faithfulness in our own lives.

Unforgiveness:

Harboring unforgiveness in our hearts is like throwing water on the fire of our prayer altar. Jesus explicitly linked forgiveness with effective prayer: "And when ye stand praying, forgive, if ye have ought against any: that your Father also which is in heaven may forgive you your trespasses" (Mark 11:25, KJV). You need to know that unforgiveness creates a blockage in our spiritual channels, hindering the flow of God's power in our prayer lives. It's a heavy burden that weighs down our spirits and distracts us from fully engaging with God in prayer. Moreover, unforgiveness often leads to bitterness, which the Bible warns can defile many (Hebrews

12:15, KJV).

To maintain a powerful prayer altar, we must regularly examine our hearts for any traces of unforgiveness and choose to forgive as Christ has forgiven us. This doesn't mean that forgiveness is always easy or that the feelings associated with hurt immediately disappear, but it does mean making a conscious decision to release the offender and trust God with the outcome.

Prayerlessness:

This might seem obvious, but one of the greatest hindrances to a powerful prayer life is simply not praying enough. Many believers fall into the trap of thinking about prayer, talking about prayer, or even studying about prayer, without engaging in the act of prayer itself. Prayerlessness can stem from various issues like busyness, laziness, doubt about prayer's effectiveness, or simply a lack of discipline. Whatever the cause, the result is the same "a weak and ineffective prayer altar". To overcome prayerlessness, we must intentionally cultivate a habit of prayer. This might involve setting specific prayer times, using prayer reminders, or integrating prayer into our daily routines. As we faithfully engage in prayer, we'll find that it becomes less of a duty and more of a delight.

Spiritual Dullness:

Spiritual dullness or insensitivity can significantly hinder the power of our prayers because this condition often develops gradually as we neglect our spiritual lives, become overly focused on worldly concerns, or allow sin to desensitize us to the things of God. The Bible says in the book of Hebrews "For when for the time ye ought to be teachers, ye have need that one teach you again which be the first principles of the oracles of God, and are become such as have need of milk, and not of strong meat. For everyone that useth milk is unskilful in the word of righteousness: for he is a babe" (Hebrews 5:12-13, KJV).

Spiritual dullness affects our prayer life by making us less sensitive to God's voice, less discerning of spiritual realities, and less passionate about spending time in God's presence. It is like trying to light a fire with damp kindling - it might catch, but it will not burn with the intensity it should. To win over spiritual dullness, we need to intentionally sharpen our spiritual senses. This involves regularly feeding on God's Word, engaging in worship, fellowshipping with other believers, and most importantly, spending quality time in God's presence through prayer.

These seven hindrances will significantly impede the power released from your prayer altar, but being aware of these potential roadblocks is the first step in overcoming them. As you diligently work to remove these hindrances and faithfully tend to your prayer altars, you will find that your prayers become more effective, your spiritual sensitivity increases, and you will continually experience a greater release of God's power in your life. it is time to heed the words of James which says "The effectual fervent prayer of a righteous man availeth much" (James 5:16, KJV), and press on towards a prayer life that truly sets our spiritual altars ablaze with the fire of God's presence and power.

Learning From Daniel And His Prayer Altar

The life of Daniel gives us a powerful example of a man who valued his prayer altar above all else, even in the face of life-threatening circumstances. His commitment to prayer, despite the challenges and opposition he faced, gives us great lessons on how we should approach our own prayer lives.

Daniel's prayer life is clearly seen when we begin form, chapter 6, at this point, Daniel had already distinguished himself among the administrators of the Persian Empire due to his exceptional qualities. The king was even planning to set him over the whole kingdom. This success was what led to jealousy among his peers, who sought to find grounds for charges against him. Because these officials knew Daniel's commitment to prayer and God, they convinced King Darius to issue an edict prohibiting prayer to any god or man except the king for thirty days, they even went further to say the penalty for disobedience was to be thrown into a den of lions. This edict was a direct attack on Daniel's prayer life, targeting the very foundation of his relationship with God.

The then tells us that Daniel's response was amazing, look at it in Daniel 6:10 (KJV): *"Now when Daniel knew that the writing was signed, he went into his house; and his windows being open in his chamber toward Jerusalem, he kneeled upon his knees three times a day, and prayed, and gave thanks before his God, as he did aforetime."*

This verse reveals several key aspects of Daniel's prayer life:

Consistency: Daniel prayed three times a day. This wasn't a new practice in response to the edict, but something he did "as he did aforetime." His prayer life was marked by regularity and discipline.

Courage: Despite knowing the consequences, Daniel continued to pray openly. His windows remained open towards Jerusalem, showing that he wasn't trying to hide his devotion to God.

Posture of Humility: Daniel "kneeled upon his knees," demonstrating his humility before God.

Focus: His windows were open "toward Jerusalem," indicating his focus on God's promises and the place of His presence.

Gratitude: Even in this challenging situation, Daniel "gave thanks before his God."

Daniel's commitment to prayer cost him dearly, He was indeed thrown into the den of lions. However, God honored Daniel's faithfulness. Daniel 6:22 (KJV) tells Daniel's testimony when the King came to check if he was still alive *"My God hath sent his angel, and hath shut the lions' mouths, that they have not hurt me: forasmuch as before him innocency was found in me; and also before thee, O king, have I done no hurt."*

This miraculous deliverance not only vindicated Daniel but also led to a national acknowledgment of the power of Daniel's God, because of this, King Darius issued another decree stating, *"That in every dominion of my kingdom men tremble and fear before the God of Daniel: for he is the living God, and steadfast for ever, and his kingdom that which shall not be destroyed, and his dominion shall be even unto the end"* (Daniel 6:26, KJV).

But Daniel's prayer life wasn't just characterized by consistency in the face of opposition, we also see his perseverance in prayer when answers seemed delayed. In Daniel chapter 10, the bible shows us that Daniel was engaged in a period of mourning and fasting that lasted three full weeks, what was he doing? He was seeking understanding about a vision he had received. At the end of these three weeks, Daniel received a visitation from an angelic being. This messenger explained the delay by saying to Daniel *"Fear not, Daniel: for from the first day that thou didst set thine heart to understand, and to chasten thyself before thy God, thy words were heard, and I am come for thy words. But the prince of the kingdom of Persia withstood me one and twenty days: but, lo, Michael, one of the chief princes, came to help me; and I remained there with the kings of Persia"* (Daniel 10:12-13, KJV).

This account provides us with several crucial insights:

Immediate Response: God heard Daniel's prayer from the very first day. The delay in the answer was not due to God's inattention or unwillingness to respond.

Spiritual Warfare: The delay was caused by opposition in the spiritual realm. This reveals that our prayers can trigger spiritual battles of which we may be unaware.

Perseverance Pays Off: Despite not seeing an immediate answer, Daniel continued in prayer and fasting for three weeks. His perseverance eventually brought breakthrough.

Heavenly Assistance: The angelic messenger received help from Michael, indicating that our prayers can mobilize heavenly forces.

These aspects of Daniel's prayer life offer us a model for our own prayer altars:

Priority

You must value your prayer lives above all else, even when faced with opposition or threats; just as Daniel continued to pray despite the king's edict, you too must prioritize your time with God regardless of societal pressures or personal consequences.

Consistency:

You need to cultivate consistency in your prayer life, Daniel's habit of praying three times a day wasn't developed overnight, NO! It was a disciplined practice that he maintained even in his high-pressure role as a government official. This consistency was what provided him with a strong foundation that sustained him in times of crisis.

Humility and Thanksgiving

Learn to approach God in your prayer altar with humility and thanksgiving; despite his elevated position, Daniel knelt in prayer and gave thanks to God. This attitude of humility and gratitude is crucial in maintaining a powerful prayer altar.

Perseverance:

You must also learn to persevere in prayer, even when you don't see immediate results because we see that Daniel's three-week period of prayer and fasting teaches us that sometimes breakthrough requires persistence. We shouldn't give up if we don't see instant answers to our prayers.

Be Aware of Spiritual Dynamics:

You must also be aware of the spiritual dynamics at play when you pray, Daniel's experience reveals that our prayers can start spiritual warfare. This understanding should motivate you to pray more fervently and persistently, knowing that your prayers are making an impact in the spiritual realm.

Daniel's prayer altar stands as a powerful testament to the impact of a dedicated prayer life. His example is a challenge for us to elevate our own prayer lives, to maintain consistency and perseverance, and to trust in the far-reaching effects of our prayers. As you seek to build and maintain your own prayer altars, I advise you to draw inspiration from Daniel's unshakable commitment to His prayer life and altar. Approach your times of prayer with the same regularity, courage, humility, focus, and gratitude that characterized Daniel's prayer life. And when you face delays or opposition, remember Daniel's perseverance and the ultimate breakthrough he experienced.

I pray that your prayer altars, just like Daniel's, will become a place of tremendous spiritual power and a place where you will consistently meet God, win spiritual warfare, and where you will continually receive break through by the hand of God in the name of Jesus.

CHAPTER SEVEN

SETTING UP
AN EFFECTIVE
AND POWERFUL
FAMILY ALTAR

Enlighten The Family

I n spiritual matters, you must tread with utmost caution and wisdom, because these things are of a delicate nature and should never be approached with ignorance If you desire to witness tangible results in your family's spiritual life. The cornerstone of establishing a potent family altar lies in the thorough education of every family member regarding its great spiritual significance, this is a process that requires patience, persistence, and great insight. This enlightenment process is important because, without a proper understanding of its essence, your family members may inadvertently dismiss, belittle, or trivialize the altar, not according it the priority it rightfully deserves in their daily lives, thereby undermining its potential to transform your family's spiritual landscape.

To effectively educate your family, you must invest considerable time and effort to elucidate the intricate workings of the spiritual realm, expounding on how altars serve as conduits for angelic mobilization and, conversely, how demonic presences can be unleashed against the unwary by malevolent agents. In this exposition, you must not neglect to illuminate the stark reality that victory in the spiritual arena is never a product of mere chance or happenstance, but rather the result of intentional, focused spiritual warfare waged through the power of a Godly Altar. It is through this consecrated space that dimensions of God's power, hitherto untapped, can be released upon your family, ushering in a new era of spiritual vitality and victory.

As you embark on this enlightening journey with your family, it is important to ground your teachings in the rich soil of Scripture because the Bible abounds with examples of the power and significance of altars in the lives of God's people. Consider, for instance, the altar-building journey of Abraham, as recounted in Genesis 12:7-8: "And the Lord appeared unto Abram, and said, Unto thy seed will I give this land: and there builded he an altar unto the Lord, who appeared unto him. And he removed from thence unto a mountain on the east of Bethel, and pitched his tent, having Bethel on the west, and Hai on the east: and there he builded an altar unto the Lord, and called upon the name of the Lord." (KJV) This passage not only shows us the historical significance of altars but also shows how they serve as points of divine encounter and worship, a revelation that should be central to your family's understanding of the altar's purpose.

Also, you must impress upon your family the power that is unleashed when we unite in prayer and worship at the altar. The synergistic effect of corporate prayer cannot be overstated, look at the word of Jesus in Matthew 18:19-20 "Again I say unto you, That if two of you shall agree on earth as touching any thing that they shall ask, it shall be done for them of my Father which is in heaven. For where two or three are gathered together in my name, there am I in the midst of them." (KJV) This divine promise shows us the amplified power of united prayer and the manifest presence of God in such gatherings, a reality that should inspire your family to approach the altar with reverence, expectation, and unity of purpose.

You should also address various aspects of spiritual warfare that your family may encounter, thereby providing them with the knowledge and tools necessary to stand firm in the face of adversity. This includes understanding the nature of spiritual attacks, recognizing the tactics of the enemy, and learning how to wield spiritual weapons effectively. The family altar is not a place of play, it is also a training ground for these spiritual disciplines and a place where your family can grow in their understanding and application of spiritual warfare principles. Psalm 144:1 "Blessed be the Lord my strength, which teacheth my hands to war, and my fingers to fight:" (KJV) emphasizing the role of divine instruction in spiritual combat and the importance of the altar as a place of spiritual preparation and empowerment.

Another important aspect is that you should teach about different prayers and their specific purposes in the believer's life. From intercessory prayer to prayers of thanksgiving, each form of communication with God serves a unique function in building and maintaining a vibrant spiritual life. The family altar provides an ideal setting for practicing and perfecting these various prayer forms, allowing each family member to grow in their ability to communicate effectively with God. As you pray these different prayer types, remind your family of the exhortation found in 1 Thessalonians 5:17-18 which says "Pray without ceasing. In every thing give thanks: for this is the will of God in Christ Jesus concerning you." (KJV)

Still on teaching your family, it is important to also emphasize the power of unity in the spiritual realm. When a family stands together in faith, presenting a united front at the altar, they become a formidable force against the powers of darkness. This unity is not merely symbolic but carries tangible spiritual weight, as illustrated in Ecclesiastes 4:12: "And if one prevail against him, two shall withstand him; and a threefold cord is not quickly broken." (KJV) This principle of spiritual synergy, powerfully manifested in the context of a family altar, should inspire your family to prioritize their time together at the altar, recognizing it as a crucial component of their spiritual strength and effectiveness.

As your family grows in their understanding of these spiritual truths, they will naturally begin to prioritize the altar in their daily lives, recognizing it not as a burdensome ritual, but as a vital lifeline for divine power and protection.

Choosing A Dedicated Space

Having laid the foundation of understanding through thorough education, the next crucial step in establishing an effective family altar is the careful selection of a dedicated space within your home. This space will serve as the focal point for your family's spiritual activities, a sanctified area where prayers ascend, study of the Word takes place, and spiritual concerns are addressed collectively. The importance of this selection process cannot be overstated, for the physical location of your altar can significantly impact its effectiveness and the family's engagement with it. When choosing the location for your family altar, several factors should be taken into consideration to ensure that it becomes a place of power and significance in your home. First and foremost, seek a space that offers a degree of privacy and seclusion, away from the main thoroughfares of your house. This separation will help create a sense of reverence and focus, allowing family members to transition mentally and spiritually as they enter the altar space. Consider areas such as a spare room, a quiet corner of the living room, or even a section of your master bedroom that can be set apart for this sacred purpose.

The Bible gives us numerous examples of individuals and groups setting aside specific locations for worship and communion with God. Recall the story of Jacob in Genesis 28:18-19: "And Jacob rose up early in the morning and took the stone that he had put for his pillows, and set it up for a pillar, and poured oil upon the top of it. And he called the name of that place Bethel: but the name of that city was called Luz at the first." (KJV) Here, Jacob consecrated a particular place where he had encountered God, recognizing the importance of having a dedicated space for spiritual encounters. Similarly, your family altar should be a place that is set apart and recognized as holy ground within your home.

As you select the location for your family altar, consider the practicality of the space in relation to your family's size and needs. It should be large enough to comfortably accommodate all family members, allowing for freedom of movement during times of prayer and worship.

Remember the words of Jesus in Matthew 18:20: "For where two or three are gathered together in my name, there am I in the midst of them." (KJV) This promise shows us the power of corporate worship and prayer, which is magnified when conducted in a space specifically dedicated to that purpose. Your family altar is not just a physical location, but a spiritual nexus where heaven and earth intersect and where the presence of God is invited and experienced in a tangible way.

As you begin to use your newly established family altar, be mindful of the need for flexibility and adaptability. While consistency in location is important for establishing routine and significance, there may be times when circumstances require you to temporarily relocate or adjust your altar space. The key is to maintain the spirit and purpose of the altar, even if its physical manifestation must change. Remember that the power of the altar lies not in the specific location, but in the hearts and intentions of those who gather there to seek God's face.

Creating A Family Prayer Routine

Having established a dedicated space for your family altar, the next crucial step in having a powerful spiritual atmosphere in your home is the creation of a well-structured family prayer routine. This routine serves as the heartbeat of your family's spiritual life because it will provide a consistent rhythm of communion with God that will shape and transform your household. The importance of establishing such a routine cannot be overstated because it is through regular and intentional engagements with the Lord that your family will experience the fullness of God's presence and power in your daily lives.

When creating your family prayer routine, it is important to approach the task with both wisdom and flexibility. You must strike a delicate balance between consistency and adaptability, ensuring that your routine is robust enough to withstand the pressures of daily life while remaining flexible enough to accommodate the ever-changing dynamics of family schedules. Begin by selecting a time that works best for all family members, taking into consideration work schedules, school commitments, and other regular activities. This may require some negotiation and compromise, but the effort invested in finding a suitable time slot will pay dividends eventually.

As you establish your routine, remember the words of the Psalmist in Psalm 55:17: "Evening, and morning, and at noon, will I pray, and cry aloud: and he shall hear my voice." (KJV) This verse shows us the importance of regular and consistent prayers throughout the day. Although it may not be possible for your entire family to gather multiple times daily, you can also draw inspiration from this principle by incorporating brief moments of prayer and meditation into various points of your day, in addition to your main family altar time. The structure of your family prayer routine should be comprehensive, encompassing various aspects of spiritual growth and communion with God.

One effective approach to structuring your family prayer routine is to assign specific focuses or themes to different days of the week. For instance, you might dedicate Mondays to prayers for personal growth and character development, Tuesdays to intercession for extended family and friends, Wednesdays to praying for your local community and church, and so on. This approach not only provides variety and prevents monotony but also ensures that your family's prayers cover a wide range of important areas over time.

As you implement your family prayer routine, also cultivate an atmosphere of expectancy and faith, encourage each family member to approach the altar with hearts open to receive from God, believing that He hears and answers prayer. Remind them of the promise found in Jeremiah 33:3: "Call unto me, and I will answer thee, and shew thee great and mighty things, which thou knowest not." (KJV) This assurance of God's responsiveness can fuel your family's devotion and inspire perseverance in prayer, even when immediate results are not visible.

While consistency is key in maintaining an effective family prayer routine, it is equally important to remain sensitive to the leading of the Holy Spirit. There may be times when God prompts you to deviate from your planned routine to address specific needs or issues that arise. So, you also have to cultivate an atmosphere of spiritual sensitivity within your family, encouraging each member to share any insights or promptings they receive during prayer times. As your family grows accustomed to the prayer routine, consider incorporating elements that encourage active participation from all members. This might include assigning distinct roles or responsibilities on a rotating basis, such as leading worship, reading Scripture, or facilitating discussion. By involving everyone in the execution of the routine, you foster a sense of ownership and investment in the family altar, making it truly a collective spiritual endeavor.

The establishment of a family prayer routine is not an overnight process, sometimes you may encounter difficulties, so be patient with yourself and your family members as you navigate the challenges of implementing and maintaining this new spiritual discipline in the family.

Create An Atmosphere Of Love Around The Prayer Altar

The final, yet crucially important aspect of establishing an effective family altar is the cultivation of an atmosphere of love that permeates every gathering and interaction at the prayer altar. This loving atmosphere will serve as the spiritual glue that binds your family together in unity and creates a conducive environment for experiencing the fullness of God's presence and power. The significance of love in your family altar cannot be overstated, for it is through love that your prayers ascend to God as a sweet-smelling savor, and it is love that enables your family to thrive in every aspect of life.

As you endeavor to create this atmosphere of love around your prayer altar, I need you to understand that this love must be intentional, demonstrative, and all-encompassing. It should not be merely a sentiment or an emotion, but a tangible force that is felt and experienced by every family member. This love should reflect the very nature of God Himself, as described in 1 John 4:16: "And we have known and believed the love that God hath to us. God is love; and he that dwelleth in love dwelleth in God, and God in him." (KJV) By cultivating this divine love within your family altar, you create a microcosm of heaven on earth, a place where God's presence is invited and manifested in powerful ways.

A very crucial aspect of cultivating love at your family altar is the practice of forgiveness and reconciliation. Even in the most harmonious families, conflicts and offenses can arise, but when such issues occur, address them promptly and lovingly at the altar, using it as a place of healing and restoration. Encourage all your family members to follow the guidance of Ephesians 4:32 which says, "And be ye kind one to another, tenderhearted, forgiving one another, even as God for Christ's sake hath forgiven you." (KJV) By making forgiveness a cornerstone of your family altar experience, you prevent bitterness and resentment from taking root and ensure that your prayers are not hindered by unresolved conflicts.

The atmosphere of love you create at your family altar should extend beyond the confines of your prayer times and permeate every aspect of your family life; this means that each family member must carry the love and unity experienced at the altar into their daily interactions, allowing it to influence their behavior and decisions throughout the day. In cultivating this atmosphere of love, you should also be mindful of the unique needs and love languages of each family member. Some may respond best to words of affirmation, while others may feel most loved through acts of service or physical touch. Take the time to understand and honor these individual preferences, ensuring that each person feels genuinely loved and valued within the family altar setting. This personalized approach to expressing love aligns with the apostle Paul's exhortation in Philippians 2:4: "Look not every man on his own things, but every man also on the things of others." (KJV)

As you consistently nurture this atmosphere of love around your prayer altar, you will find that it becomes a catalyst for spiritual growth and transformation within your family. The love experienced at the altar will spill over into every area of your lives, influencing your relationships, decisions, and interactions with the world around you. Your family will become a powerful testimony to the transformative power of God's love, drawing others to the warmth and unity they witness in your home.

As you faithfully nurture this loving atmosphere, you will witness the gradual but profound impact it has on every aspect of your family's life, drawing you closer to God and to one another in ways that will leave an indelible mark on your spiritual lives for generations to come.

When you have successfully done all these you will begin to see tremendous results that are functional and powerful enough to orchestrate supernatural interventions in your life in dramatic ways.

CONCLUSION

An Altar, both in your family and in your personal life, stands as your greatest tool for survival in this wicked world, for it possesses the power to unleash God's might in every area of your existence and ensure your consistent victory in spiritual warfare. The knowledge you have now acquired about altars must not remain theoretical; it must be put into practice with an unshakable faith, dedication, and fervent zeal. The implementation of this knowledge is where the true power lies. As you step out to put your altar knowledge to work, I want you to approach this task with a sense of urgency and determination. The spiritual realm is not a playground but a battlefield, and your altar is your command center in this cosmic warfare.

Once again, remember Ephesians 6:12: "For we wrestle not against flesh and blood, but against principalities, against powers, against the rulers of the darkness of this world, against spiritual wickedness in high places." (KJV) This verse shows us the gravity of the spiritual warfare you face and the critical role your altar plays in equipping you for this battle.

To effectively put your altar knowledge to work, begin by establishing a consistent practice of altar-building in your daily life. This goes beyond merely setting aside a physical space; it involves cultivating a mindset of constant communion with God; I am saying, make it a habit to create mini altars throughout your day "moments of focused prayer, praise, and spiritual reflection amidst your daily activities." These spiritual touch points will help you serve to maintain a constant relationship with the lord, ensuring that the power of your altar is not confined to a specific time or place but permeates every aspect of your life.

In your family, do not allow the devil to rob you of the power of altars, your family altar must be strong fervent, and burning with power. The Lord does not want any member of your family to be a casualty of demonic altars, and neither does he intend for any of you to fall in destiny.

As you apply your altar knowledge, be prepared for opposition and challenges because the enemy of your soul recognizes the power of an active altar and will attempt to discourage, distract, and derail your efforts to maintain it both in your life and in your family. In such times, recall the determination of Nehemiah, who declared in Nehemiah 6:3, "I am doing a great work, so that I cannot come down: why should the work cease, whilst I leave it, and come down to you?" (KJV) Let this resolute spirit characterize your approach to your altar, refusing to abandon or neglect it in the face of adversity or competing demands.

The knowledge you have gained about altars is a priceless treasure, but its true value is realized only when put into action.

It's time to start building and it's time to experience power!

A SPECIAL CALL TO SALVATION & NEW BEGINNINGS FROM APOSTLE DR. DAVID PHILEMON

Dear Beloved,

God loves you deeply and has brought you to this moment for a reason. No matter your past, His love and forgiveness are available to you.

The Bible says in John 3:16, "For God so loved the world that He gave His one and only Son, that whoever believes in Him shall not perish but have eternal life." Jesus Christ came to save you, offering you a new life of purpose and peace.

If you're ready to accept Jesus as your Lord and Savior, pray this simple prayer:

The Salvation Prayer

"Heavenly Father, I come to You in the Name of Jesus. I acknowledge that I am a sinner in need of a Savior. I believe that

Jesus Christ is Your Son, that He died for my sins, and that You raised Him from the dead. I repent of my sins and turn to You with my

Whole heart. Jesus, I ask You to come into my life. Be my Lord and my Savior. I surrender my life to You. Fill me with Your Holy Spirit, guide me on the path of righteousness, and help me to follow Your script for my life. Thank you, Father, for saving me. In the name of Jesus. Amen."

Welcome to the Family of God!

If you have just prayed this prayer, Congratulations! You are now a child of God, and heaven is rejoicing. Your journey has begun, and we're here to support you as you grow in faith and discover God's unique plans for you.

Next Steps:

• Connect with a Bible-believing church.

• Read the Bible Daily: God's Word is your guide.

• Pray Regularly: Prayer is your lifeline to God.

• Share Your Faith: Don't keep the good news to yourself.

www.ingramcontent.com/pod-product-compliance
Lightning Source LLC
Chambersburg PA
CBHW071904020426
42331CB00010B/2667